On the Idea of a University
J.M. CAMERON

J. M. CAMERON is a member of the Department of Philosophy at Saint Michael's College in the University of Toronto, and a frequent contributor to the *New York Review of Books*.

Starting from Newman's concept of the university as a place of liberal education, Professor Cameron examines how today's university functions, what its aims should be and what its strengths and deficiencies are, and presents some proposals for reform. He argues that liberal education, in which knowledge is pursued for its own sake as well as for the advantages it may bring, should remain the core of university studies, although he emphasizes that natural science and the technologies, as well as the traditional arts subjects, may be studied liberally in the university. In the course of a rich and broad-ranging discussion, he singles out parasensical discourse — a kind of curious verbal play, neither sense nor nonsense, designed to inculcate attitudes, not convey information — as a symptom of the crisis in the university today. Cameron's trenchant analysis of it and of the serious ills that it represents is particularly relevant to an understanding of the controversy surrounding modern university education.

The four lectures in this volume were originally delivered to mark the sesquicentennial of the University of Toronto and the 125th anniversary of Saint Michael's College. The occasion, Cameron writes, 'gave me a chance to consider the nature and spirit of the institution within which I have spent most of my working life.'

At a time when the value of university education is being questioned, Cameron provides a fresh perspective on the university's purpose, its form, and its future. The volume is published in association with the University of Saint Michael's College by University of Toronto Press.

J.M. CAMERON

On the Idea of a University

PUBLISHED IN ASSOCIATION WITH
THE UNIVERSITY OF SAINT MICHAEL'S COLLEGE
BY UNIVERSITY OF TORONTO PRESS
TORONTO BUFFALO LONDON

Canadian Cataloguing in Publication Data

Cameron, James M., 1910–
    On the idea of a university

    Lectures delivered on the occasion of the 150th
    birthday of the University of Toronto and the
    125th birthday of St. Michael's College.

    ISBN 0-8020-2300-2 bd.   ISBN 0-8020-6335-7 pa.

    1. Universities and colleges – Addresses,
    essays, lectures. I. Title.

    LB2325.C35   378   C78-001005-1

DUNCE IN BOCARDO*

He stands in the violet shadow
By the scribbled wall
And sticks his finger in every Tudor eye.

The pen is dry, the shadow
Is deeper, the fool
Quits the sleeping prince.

Cranmer's pears are sleepy, Pole
In Westminster nibbles Luther, heretics
Are sword-swallowers, eaters of fire.

In the apple-tree the. blackbird
Whistles his belief, tailors
Catch snails, huntsmen chase
The owl in the holly-tree.

Now comes the violet night, the lewd
Citizens creep, then run, then
Snatch at glosses in blind corners

And kisses: Grape Street is dark.
From grope to grape by Bowdler's Law,†
Then back to grope by *ius positivum.*

Sweet Isis, you run softly
Through the future's unimagin
able inscape

Id quod oculis meis vidi.

* Wee have set Dunce in Bocardo, (a prison so called) and have utterly banished
  him Oxford for ever, with all his blynd glosses, and is now made a common servant to every man, fast nayled up upon posts in all common howses of easement,
  id quod oculis meis vidi ... (Richard Layton to Thomas Cromwell).
† My friend Professor W.G. Hoskins first drew my attention to this application of
  Bowdler's Law.

Contents

Foreword

When Universities and Colleges reach a relatively mature age they do not think of dying but rather of renewing their youth. Historical change, while constant, should do something other than induce immediate staleness. This is particularly true when the life which changes is that of the mind and spirit. Perhaps the late Jacques Maritain would agree that to some extent education is always at a crossroads.

Entering the last quarter of the twentieth century it seems that the University of Toronto and Saint Michael's College have indeed come to a major crossroads. Which turn do we take to ensure that we renew our youth? Which steps do we take to revitalize our union?

The University of Toronto is rethinking her goals as she celebrates her 150th birthday. Saint Michael's is searching for new ways to fulfill her purpose as she passes her 125th year. Both tasks require the reflection of a philosopher. Both institutions are extremely fortunate that James Cameron has agreed to help in this work of renewal by giving these lectures that take as their starting point Newman's work and stimulate our thinking about the major problems in university education today.

JOHN M. KELLY C.S.B.

Preface

Institutions have in some sense minds and identities that persist through time, though their secure possession needs to be continually asserted, like a public right to gather firewood or graze a goose on common land, if it is to be maintained. And institutions can die. This seems to justify my taking yet another look at Newman's *The Idea of a University*, the most influential (I suppose) book yet written on university education. The occasion of my looking was, as President Kelly notes in the Fore-word to this book, the 150th birthday of the University of Toronto and the 125th birthday of Saint Michael's College. I was invited by the Col-lege to contribute to the celebration of these events by delivering a set of lectures on some of the problems now troubling the university world. The following pages are a record of these lectures. What is printed is sub-stantially what I said, though I have made some changes in the wording and removed and added material here and there. I am grateful to Father John M. Kelly, President of Saint Michael's College, for his constant encouragement, and to those colleagues who looked after the publicity for the lectures; their efforts were handsomely rewarded, and I therefore owe thanks to them and to the many who came through those four February nights to listen to me. No lecturer could have had a more cordial reception.

My first years as a teacher were spent in adult education; and I have come to think that my notions about liberal education were much affected by those years. Adult men and women who study philosophy or literature or history with no anxious reaching after qualifications or professional advantages are in that respect the ideal students of Newman's dream of liberal education. Also, they can always vote with their feet and leave the class; and thus they test the teacher's art. Such students also bring out the way in which liberal education is founded upon what I have dared to call a 'natural' relationship between teacher and taught. I am grateful, therefore, to all those students, members of the Workers' Educational Association in Great Britain and others, from whose experience and forbearance and active sympathy I have profited, as I am also grateful for the friendship and support of so many colleagues and pupils at the Universities of Leeds, Kent, and Toronto, and in the United States, at the University of Notre Dame.

In what follows I have rough words for some sides of education in the humanities in many universities, the University of Toronto included, in North America. I am reminded by colleagues that some of the things I find missing from the present regimen here and some of the things I should like to see supplied were in fact features of the old order displaced by what was called, when I came here in 1971, the New Programme. Further, I had assumed without much thought that the New Programme was in its general character prescribed by the recommendations of the Macpherson Committee.* I realize now that while that Committee's recommendations about the colleges and college departments were a portent of the changes now taking place, its recommendations about the degree programmes, which would have retained structured specialist and

---

* *Undergraduate Instruction in Arts and Science.* Report of the Presidential Advisory Committee on Undergraduate Instruction in the Faculty of Arts and Science, University of Toronto, 1967.

generalist degrees, were quite unlike the cafeteria or free-elective arrangement that was inaugurated by the New Programme. On the relation of teaching and examinations, the spirit of the Report is admirable. In particular the authors of the Report want to free the undergraduate from routine and rote learning and from the practice of regurgitating, in examinations and other written exercises, material given in lectures or dredged from some muddy textbook. My own view is that for such benefits to be had it is necessary to make greater changes than the Committee felt able to propose; and some recommendations on specific points were, I think, contrary to the ethos the Committee wanted to commend.

I wish to thank Mrs Audrey McDonagh and Mrs Aruna Alexander of Saint Michael's College for secretarial help and Dr R.M. Schoeffel of University of Toronto Press for other kinds of help and advice. Mr T.F. Burns, the Editor of *The Tablet*, has kindly allowed me to quote at length from the sermon preached by Father Peter Levi at the Requiem Mass for David Jones. The poem *Dunce in Bocardo* I use as an epigraph was first published in *Rune*. My wife has patiently sustained me during the composition of the lectures and their redaction.

J.M.C.
Saint Michael's College
September 1977

ON THE IDEA OF A UNIVERSITY

I

The Idea of a University Revisited

To go back to the text of the discourses collected into *The Idea of a University* is to travel backwards in time. I choose then to begin with some reflections, general and personal, on the past and on those questions that gather round us as we try to understand Newman's thought, and to think it again, so far as this is possible (and profitable). One who was born before 1914, as this writer was, and who has survived into the 1970s, has a strong sense, not only that he is moving towards the end of his own life, but that an entire world is coming to an end. The war through which I lived as a child will always remain for me the *Great* War. I came to my maturity in the age of the great tyrannies and the great massacres. I have lived through many technological revolutions. I read my first books by the light of candles or oil lamps or under the hissing gas-jet. I remember the horse as a common means of local traction and transport and the sharp smell of the streets as the great Shires and Clydesdales staled upon the cobblestones. I remember the coming of radio broadcasting. I was moving through middle age when the first computers appeared. When I first came from England to North America I came by ship. My early summers were loud with the noise of millions of insects, few of them noxious, most of them useful or beautiful. My intention here, and my reason for inserting this piece of my own history, is to establish a sense of the gaps between worlds and times.

Many in the last hundred years or so have had the thought not so much that their own personal world was dying – a world dies with each generation – but that with the establishment of industrialism and the victory of clock-time and the secular kalendar over the time set by the sun and the seasons and the ecclesiastical kalendar, with the movement from a society living in part by oral traditions to one in which most people can read and write, there was an evident break with a culture stretching far back into the human past, back even to the world of the *Iliad* and of the earliest warriors, shepherds, and cultivators of the soil.

Lest this be thought an exaggeration, I add, as an illustration of the point, another fragment from the recollections of a man born before 1914. My father, who was born in 1880, served in the first World War, and died in 1967, remembered as a boy in the West Highlands of Scotland the coming to his home – a group of poor crofts growing potatoes and raising a few sheep and cattle and nourished by the fish taken from Loch Linnhe – of a blind man who would, in exchange for a bed and modest entertainment, recite long epics in the Gaelic language. Thus, a man, living in the 1970s, has through his father, born in 1880, touched the world of Homer.

But why does the story of the blind reciter of epic raise, as it were spontaneously, the name of Homer? There seems something paradoxical here. That we know about worlds that now exist primarily in oral traditions is a consequence of their destruction and the rise of the literate civilizations. That the world of Homer or of the Icelandic sagas is still alive in the modern world is a consequence, not so much of the work of textual scholars and of historians, as of the transmission of that culture we call humanism, the cultivation of an interest in the classical literary texts, an interest surviving through the Dark and Middle Ages into the modern world, a culture that with the growth of historical and philological interest in the vernacular cultures found the genre of epic, first encountered in Homer, in the dark past of the northern peoples of Europe. In the transmission of this culture the universities, institutions that are from the beginning concerned with the liberal arts, that is, with the study of language (grammar) and *therefore* with the study and exercise of the imagination and with the re-creation and understanding of the past, are thus a part of the line – truly, I believe, a life-line – that joins us to the entire human past, so far as this is recoverable, and it is only through our knowing whence we have come that we know who and what we are. If our society suffers from what is in modern jargon called an identity crisis (perhaps it ought rather to be called a quiddity crisis), it is because this line is frayed though not perhaps quite cut. Newman brings out with great art the ways in which we find ourselves in studying the literature of the past.

> Passages [from some classical author], which to a boy are but rhetorical commonplaces ... at length come home to him, when long years have passed, and he has had experience of life, and pierce him ... with their sad earnestness and vivid exactness. Then he comes to understand how it is that lines, the birth of some chance morning or evening at an Ionian festival, or among the Sabine hills, have lasted generation after generation, for thousands of years, with a power over the mind, and a charm, which the current literature of his own day, with all its obvious advantages, is utterly unable to rival. Perhaps this is the reason of the medieval opinion about Virgil, as if a prophet or magician; his single words and phrases, his pathetic half-lines, giving utterance, as the voice of Nature herself, to that pain and weariness, yet hope of better things, which is the experience of her children in every time.[1]

Men of the nineteenth and early twentieth centuries belong both to the primeval and to the civilized worlds, both to the oral and to the written culture, both to the way of life founded upon handicraft and local trade and to the way of life determined by machine manufacture and the world market. Many have felt the poignancy of this situation, the divided feelings, the aching nostalgia for the past of the old ballads and tales of long ago, the burning hopes for the future, hopes that have their own sad flavour since we know, deep in our minds, that *these* will not be realized; whatever, good or evil, is to come, it won't be what we expect. Thomas Hardy built such feelings into the greatest of his novels, *The Mayor of Casterbridge, The Return of the Native, Tess of the D'Urbervilles.* Far away in the East the same note of feeling is unmistakably struck in the work of Chekhov. Péguy in his autobiographical fragment *Notre Jeunesse* cries out: 'Nous sommes les derniers!' – We are the last of all! Some of the charm of Proust's great novel comes from the evocation of an older France embedded in the vocabulary and forms of speech of the servant Françoise.

The culture such men found at home and in school, in the library and the bookshop, was the culture of what is sometimes called 'humanism.' It was given its form and its seminal ideas by the philosophers, poets and historians of ancient Greece and Rome, of the Middle Ages, of the revival of classical learning, and by the novelists, historians, poets, scientists, of the centuries since then. For much of the period it lived, sometimes amicably, sometimes uneasily, with the Biblical culture that is now so thin that it may be on the point of vanishing. We begin to discover, with distress, that some of the most intelligent of those we teach in the universities have, for some reason we can't pick out with any certainty, either lost, substantially, this culture, or look upon it in an essentially external way: it does not strike them as a powerful instrument for the interpretation of human life.

How much of all this has gone tends to be underestimated in the countries of Anglo-Saxon Protestant tradition, perhaps as a consequence of their identifying Christianity with the morality of the good citizen; to say of a man that he is not a Christian is not to say that he disbelieves the Apostles' Creed but to suggest that he may be given to robbery or wife-stealing. Perhaps, too, we fail to notice that the strain of religiosity common in much public exhortation masks a drying-up of our religious tradition. We are no longer surprised or disturbed when fashionable preachers and teachers embrace the very corruptions of our society as instances of bold moral pioneering. The capitulation before the world of

Christian spokesmen in matters of sexual morality is as startling, though it will soon be as familiar, as the capitulation of earlier generations of ecclesiastics to the claims of capitalism and of the modern nation state.

In looking back, then, or, more strongly, in returning to Newman's writings on university subjects, both those included in *The Idea of a University* and those, almost as remarkable, originally published in 1856 as *The Office and Work of Universities* and later collected in the third volume of *Historical Sketches* (1876), we are returning to a world, a way of thinking and feeling about man and human society, the human past and the human future, that no longer has any great purchase upon many of those who are now in the full vigour of their adult life, though most men born before 1914 feel close to it. If what Newman has to say to us, across the chasm of almost 130 years, is to be commended, it must be on its own merits, not just as a classic of English prose to which we give a respectful nod in passing. We must apply to Newman the tests we apply to, say, a work by Matthew Arnold. *Culture and Anarchy* certainly belongs to its period and there is much in it to make us smile and some things to irritate us; but most readers would think there is that in it which speaks to us in our own time. Like the educational writings of Newman, it is a piece of Victorian writing immersed in contemporary problems; it can be said to speak to us in so far as it penetrates below the particularities that belong to its time and brings out what is of permanent interest.

The discourses to be found in the first part of *The Idea* were delivered in 1852 as a consequence of Newman's having been invited to preside over the construction of a Catholic university in Dublin and to be its first Rector. Like all Newman's best writings, they are addressed to a particular occasion; but, as always, he uses the opportunity of the occasion to expound what he thinks to be arguments and considerations of general importance. To us there is something both comical and sad in the spectacle of Newman, so graceful and delicate, the most exquisite product of Tractarian Oxford, striving to convince the Irish Catholics, bishops, gentry, middle class, that a university is neither a seminary for the laity to be run by clergy who will always be wiser and better instructed than their charges nor a useful institution to be judged by its power to bring about the material betterment of Irish society. (It is easy to forget how near Newman's discourses are to the great famine of the 'forties.) This was not the time or the place for such a venture. The prospect of building Louvain (at that time perhaps the only really flourishing Catholic university in western Europe) on the banks of the Liffey was illusory. Slowly Newman came to see this. If he was sometimes tempted to think that all would have been different had Archbishop Cullen of Dublin been warm and frank – he was cold and devious and solved the problem presented to him by Newman by not replying to his letters – or the great Archbishop McHale less of a lion and more of a lamb (it was McHale's peculiarity that he suspected Newman of designing to establish Oxford on the banks of the Liffey), he came in the end to see that nothing great could come of his work in that place and at that time. Something great did nevertheless come of it, though it was not to be a great institution; it was rather the most penetrating and in many respects the most influential treatment, in the English language and in modern times, of the theory of the university. We now know through the work of historians much more about the actual functioning of the great variety of institutions called universities than Newman did. More was known in 1852 about the Greek *polis* and the Roman Empire than was known about the university as an institution having an instructive history. But Newman had the incomparable advantage of having been an initiator of the first stages of reform in nineteenth-century Oxford; of having been at the heart of an institution he loved and was to go on loving all his life; and of being able through his command of language to communicate to later generations his first perception that essentially 'a University is an intellectual power, as such'; and as such a power likely to be from time to time obnoxious to the national State, always jealous of powers that exist over against it and have claims to the exercising of an independent authority. He was to come to know in the course of his long and in some respects frustrated life as a Catholic, that the intellectual independence of even a friendly critic may be in the same way and for similar reasons irritating to ecclesiastical authority.

All the arguments in *The Idea* are worth attention. I propose to pick out two themes: what Newman has to say about 'liberal' education; and

what he thinks to be the role of literary studies, broadly understood as
including much history and some of what we now call philosophy.

The term 'liberal education' has a complicated history. One sense,
and this is the predominant one and the one that stands behind Newman's use of the term, is that of an education suitable for free men as
contrasted with men who are enslaved, or are preoccupied with getting
their bread by hard physical work, or are absorbed in commerce. Liberal
education goes with a certain largeness in the style of life of teacher and
taught; material cares are assumed to be, if not altogether banished, at
least not to be too consuming; the life of liberal study is free of perpetual
occupation with small tasks, with concern about means to unconsidered
ends, that is, it is a life of leisure, though by no means a life of idleness.
Newman's irritation with the counterfeit of liberal education offered in
his own day vents itself on occasion, and the vigour of his comment
brings out what, in his view, liberal education is not. In one such passage
he begins by arguing that self-education has great imperfections, in part
because the autodidact does not engage in the interchange of ideas which
goes with living in a society of students and teachers; he thus may be
'too often ignorant of what everyone knows and takes for granted, of
that multitude of small truths which fall upon the mind like dust, im-
palpable and ever accumulating';[2] but such drawbacks are as nothing
compared with the state of

> those earnest but ill-used persons, who are forced to load their
> minds with a score of subjects against an examination, who have
> too much on their hands to indulge themselves in thinking or in-
> vestigation, who devour premiss and conclusion together with in-
> discriminate greediness, who hold whole sciences on faith, and
> commit demonstrations to memory, and who too often, as might
> be expected, when their period of education is passed, throw up
> all they have learned in disgust, having gained nothing really by
> their anxious labours, except, perhaps, the habit of application.[3]

Far better to be an autodidact than the half-educated product of so bar-
barous a system.

How much better ... for the active and thoughtful intellect, where such is to be found, to eschew the College and the University altogether, than to submit to a drudgery so ignoble, a mockery so contumelious! How much more profitable for the independent mind, after the mere rudiments of education, to range through a library at random, taking down books as they meet him, and pursuing the trains of thought which his mother wit suggests! ... How much more genuine an education is that of the poor boy in the Poem* who ... contrived from the beach, and the quay, and the fisher's boat, and the inn's fireside, and the tradesman's shop, and the shepherd's walk, and the smuggler's hut, and the mossy moor, and the screaming gulls, and the restless waves, to fashion for himself a philosophy and a poetry of his own.[4]

An even apter example for Newman's purposes, and a real one, would have been William Cobbett† whose projected but never completed account of his own life was to have been entitled 'The Progress of a Ploughboy to a seat in Parliament.' Cobbett resolved to bring up his children in the country just because rural life had been for him one great means of education somewhat on the pattern suggested by Newman as preferable to the ignoble drudgery of a system ruled by examinations.

When I was a little boy, I was, in the barley-sowing season, going along by the side of a field, near Waverley Abbey; the primroses and bluebells new spangling the banks on both sides of me; while the jingle of the traces and the whistling of the plough-boys saluted my ears over the hedge; and, as it were to snatch me from the enchantment, the hounds, at that instant, having started a hare in the hanger on the other side of the field, came scampering over it in full cry, taking me after them many a mile. I was not more than eight years old; but this particular scene presented itself to

---

* The reference is to the Rev. George Crabbe, *Tales of the Hall*, 2 vols., London, 1819, Vol. 1, pp. 74ff.

† In our own day Neville Cardus would be a good example. See his *Autobiography*, London, 1947.

my mind every year from that day. I always enjoyed it over again; and I was resolved to give, if possible, the same enjoyments to my children.[5]

What this singular man achieved for his children was the establishment of a little republic of letters, one which shows how slightly we are dependent, if we have courage to act on our convictions and good fortune in our callings, on subventions or other helps from public authorities. He writes:

Children naturally want to be like their parents, and do what they do; and as I was always writing or reading, mine naturally desired to do something in the same way. Fond of book-learning ... I naturally wished them to possess it too; but never did I impose it upon any one of them.

I accomplished my purpose indirectly. Health was secured by the deeply interesting and never-ending sports of the field and pleasures of the garden. Luckily these things were treated of in books and pictures of endless variety; so that, on wet days, in long evenings, these came into play. A large strong table in the middle of the room, their mother sitting at her work, used to be surrounded with them, the baby, if big enough, set up in a high chair. Here were inkstands, pens, pencils, indiarubber, and paper, all in abundance and everyone scrabbled about as he or she pleased. There were prints of animals of all sorts; books treating of them; others treating of gardening, of flowers, of husbandry, of hunting, coursing, shooting, fishing, planting. ... One would be trying to imitate a bit of my writing, another drawing the pictures of some of our horses and dogs, a third poking over Bewick's 'Quadrupeds,' and picking out what he said about them; but our book of never-failing resource was the 'Maison Rustique' which, it is said, was the book that first tempted Dusquenois, the famous physician, in the reign of Louis XIV, to learn to read. And there was I, in my leisure moments, to join this inquisitive group, to read the French, and tell them what it meant in English.[6]

Looking at Cobbett's small good society does not carry us so far from the topic of liberal education as might be thought. It would not be too far outside our purpose if we were to note Cobbett's small republic as a preparation for and a foundation of any later enterprise, likely to succeed, in education. Of course, the specific details of Cobbett's scheme are not in question. There are all the same clear principles that come out of the details: the grouping is 'natural,' not a chance coming together of persons related only externally (this is the principle that an educational enterprise is quasi-familial or collegiate); the impulse to learn comes from the desire to imitate models, in this case the father, offered by older people and from a natural curiosity prompted by the way they live; the father – the teacher – has a 'natural' authority, he acts as a president rather than as a despotic ruler, and as he knows more than the children (he is better equipped to set the curriculum) they can learn from him what they could not – and this is the strong 'could not' of logic – learn for themselves, in this case writing and the French language. The whole is pursued in the spirit of freedom, and in this it *is* a liberal education in miniature: 'everyone scrabbled about as he or she pleased.'

It follows from the sense of liberal education so far set out that certain subjects will be liberal, others not. In a society where some are free and leisured, others either enslaved or preoccupied with physical labour or business, anything necessarily connected with the occupations of slaves, manual workers, business men, will be inappropriate. This is the assumption of Plato and Aristotle; and it passes over into the modern world through the medieval and renaissance writers. This would mean, to transpose the problem into the terms of our own society, that philosophy, mathematics, speculative physics, the *theory* of music, would all be suitable constituents of a curriculum of liberal studies; but that cookery, carpentry, book-binding, singing, piano-playing, bookkeeping, surgery would not. (There are some curious, as it would seem to us, anomalies in the Greek lists: military strategy and the art of war generally is accounted a liberal study, though it seems as much directed to an end beyond itself as any of the subjects associated with servility or drudgery. Irrelevant associations seem to close in upon us here, as when we find the man on the horse noble, the man on a donkey a little comic, Sancho Panza or proletarian holiday-maker on the spree.) Now, it would seem ridiculous to keep such a sense of liberal education, liberal studies, in our society. The institution of chattel slavery has been given up, and it seems plain that in our day the concentration of intense thought upon problems within industry is such that it would be very curious to banish the useful subjects from higher education. As to the thought that playing the flute and surgery are essentially servile occupations, this seems as strange to us as does the excommunication of actors and actresses in seventeenth-century France.

But perhaps there is some deeper sense of liberal education that will allow us to keep the archaic sense and yet not talk absurdly. Newman must have thought so, for thinking as he did that the university is essentially a place of liberal studies, he sought to establish 'a medical school, a school of useful or industrial sciences, an archaeological department with a Press; and, in like manner, an *Observatory*.'[7] He commends these institutions or schools as valuable in themselves and commanding respect, 'while the real University (i.e. the bodies and minds of its constituents,) is growing in number and in intellect under their shadow.'[8] Plainly this is in his estimation no blighting shadow, no Upas tree.

Newman argues that liberal studies, or subjects studied in a liberal spirit, have two marks. The study concerned is worth pursuing for its own sake; there is no need to justify it by pointing to ends that lie beyond it; it may also be good as instrumental to some further good, but it may be taken as good in itself. Further, though liberal knowledge is worth having for its own sake, it does in practice have an effect upon the characters of men; it tends to produce a special kind of man, that great exemplar of civility, the gentleman.

Many have difficulty with the idea that education at its finest consists in a set of speculative activities that are not to be justified by their being directly useful to society or by their tendency to further the betterment of mankind. Education is today so often discussed in a high-minded rhetoric that the notion that at its most intense education is not concerned with the social good, does not serve – or rather is not designed to serve – purposes that go beyond the activities in which education consists, seems almost a kind of nonsense. Why do we pay taxes and solicit gifts from rich men for the maintaining of universities if they are to be retreats in which a small, self-centred élite (ah, how the word *élite* stings today!) may take its pleasures? Such would be a common political response and it is quite understandable.

Almost anything can be pursued for its own sake, even pain or postage stamps. The pursuit of pain or postage stamps has to be given a special justification, for the function of pain is to warn us about something, the function of postage stamps is to facilitate paying for the carriage of our correspondence. Consequently, while masochism and philately can be explained, they do need to be explained, just because of what pain is and of what postage stamps are; and it seems clear that not all men could be masochistic in relation to all pains – this is not a possible picture of human life – and that philately would lose its point if it were not normal to buy stamps to stick on letters. Why men go in for pain or for collecting postage stamps not to stick on letters is a question that seems always to be in order.

But there seem to be other objects, or states of mind, or experiences, that characteristically repel the question *why* with some authority. *Why do you spend time listening to Rosalyn Tureck playing the 48 Preludes and Fugues of Johann Sebastian Bach?* is in some though not all circumstances a strange question and a man might well be stumped for an answer, if the peremptoriness with which the question was put were to scare him into thinking he was bound to give an answer. Of course, an answer could be given: It is for the sake of acquiring the virtue of temperance (this would have pleased Plato); I am trying to forget an unhappy love; I am trying to impress my superiors. All these answers make good sense. But such responses are not *demanded* by the nature of the activity, as they are demanded when a man is seeking pain or collects postage stamps for his own delight. It seems just obvious that a part of life can be given to the music of Bach without the giving having to be justified. It is possible to say: Why do you spend so much time listening to the music of Bach while your children are down-at-heel and hungry? But this is not to deny that listening to such music is a good thing in itself; it only becomes subject to criticism if the listener's duties are grossly neglected. It does not seem true that anyone ever has a *duty* to listen to Bach; listening to Bach seems much more like exercising a right than fulfilling a duty. This means that we may sometimes have a duty to put people in the way of listening to Bach (or any other liberal activity). Parents of gifted children notoriously have, other things being equal, such duties. *

There are, then, activities which characteristically repel the question *Why are you doing that?* with some authority. And Newman thinks that those activities which are the core of a liberal education at the level of the university are among them. 'Knowledge is capable of being its own end. Such is the constitution of the human mind, that any kind of knowledge, if it really be such, is its own reward.'[9] While such knowledge is often taken to be restricted to the traditional subjects of the humanities curriculum, it need not be so. Chemistry, anatomy, and engineering, as well as literature, history, and philosophy, are matters of knowledge, and there is no reason why we should decide on *a priori* grounds that such knowledge cannot be pursued for its own sake. Indeed, one might say that the difference between the study of such subjects at the university level and their study in vocational schools is that in the former case the study is *liberal*. Any university department that conducted its assigned studies primarily as vocational skills to serve practical ends would soon find that it was stagnating or getting worse. In any case, the world seems so to be arranged that a passionate curiosity unaffected by any desire for practical results does in fact produce, without aiming at it, results that are useful by the standards of the world. Who would have conjectured that Rutherford had death in his hand, that refined speculations on the nucleus of the atom would help to undo so many lives, in a moment, at Hiroshima and Nagasaki? Nuclear weapons are eminently prac-

---

* For Newman's thought, liberal studies are not indispensable means to fullness of life. To think so would be to approach Newman with presuppositions drawn from our own intellectual milieu. Newman thought a perfectly satisfactory life could be lived by those who were without the gifts and experience to make liberal studies profitable. He viewed the characteristic product of liberal education with some reserve, and his treatment of this product, the gentleman, is ironical. The gentleman may be so far as he goes a remarkable thing, but he never illustrates the greatest elevation human nature is capable of.

tical devices, though they come out of the (to the layman) Alice-through-the-looking-glass world of sub-atomic physics.

Newman's argument is not that liberal studies in which men take knowledge to be its own end do not have consequences of importance to individual persons and to society. Apart from those consequences, such as we have just looked at, that come to the world through the speculative study of the structure of matter, any study is bound to have effects upon the student and any society may inquire whether or not it wants to encourage the growth of a certain kind of character. Newman argues that in fact liberal education does tend to produce a certain kind of man, 'the gentleman.' Our inverted snobbery is now so great that it is hard even to utter the word 'gentleman' (or the word 'lady'), except as a joke. In a forgotten American novel of the 1870s,[10] written to encourage total abstinence, self-reliance, hard work, and undenominational Protestant Christianity, one of the chapters is entitled 'Is he a Gentleman?' It seemed important that the central character of an improving novel be shown to be a gentleman. (His gentility is demonstrated rather curiously, by his ability to read music at sight.) This seems scarcely imaginable today.

However, the character of the gentleman as Newman conceives it has little to do with the social attitudes that in our day make the word almost unusable.

> Liberal Education makes not the Christian, not the Catholic but the gentleman. It is well to be a gentleman, it is well to have a cultivated intellect, a delicate taste, a candid, equitable dispassionate mind, a noble and courteous bearing in the conduct of life; – they are the connatural qualities of a large knowledge; they are the objects of a University; ... but still ... they are no guarantee for sanctity, or even for conscientiousness, for they may attach to the man of the world, to the profligate, to the heartless. ... Quarry the granite rock with razors, or moor the vessel with a thread of silk; then may you hope with such keen and delicate instruments as human knowledge and human reason to contend against those giants, the passion and the pride of man.[11]

Liberal education, that is, is not salvation in any of the senses of salvation. Newman, like Hume before him, and like the Duke of Wellington and Karl Marx, his contemporaries, is arguing against the Enlightenment view that giving people information or intellectual skills will in itself bring it about that their practical judgments are wise. This would be true if it were a common characteristic of men that they are motivated by rational self-interest. Manifestly this is not generally true. It is astonishing that so many of those professionally concerned with education cling to this strange belief, strange, at any rate, at a time when Freud and Marx are major intellectual influences and when this prejudice of the Enlightenment can be retained only against the plain lessons of experience. Those who are experienced in the counselling of young people know that the best informed about sexuality are not on that account the most prudent and temperate. Of course, ignorance does not produce these virtues either.

Nevertheless, liberal education is a good thing, not as such conducive to the moral virtues but a part of the virtue of civility; and it would be absurd to chide it because it is not good for everything. Everything is what it is and not another thing, as the good Bishop Butler said. I am satisfied that in none of its senses can salvation come from the university's discharging its proper task, if this is, as I shall assume it is, the provision of liberal education. I do not argue that enlightenment, knowing how things are with the world and men, is something idle and frivolous. Prudent judgments cannot be made in a fog of ignorance; knowing the limits of liberal education is itself a virtue of the liberally educated man, just as it is also one of his virtues that he does not require of any particular subject of discourse a degree of precision that cannot belong to the subject. And it may well be the case that the presence within society of liberally educated persons is a catalyst, in the strict and not the fashionable jargon sense of the word, for processes from which good things may be hoped for. I believe this *is* so, as I shall urge later. Newman himself, after having smitten the spokesmen of the Utilitarian doctrine and left them bleeding, if not dying, on the field, goes on in his seventh Discourse ('Knowledge viewed in relation to Professional Skill') to argue that if intellectual culture is the health of the mind, then we may expect good

things to come of it, just as we expect good things to come of the health
of the body, even though bodily health would in itself be a good thing
if nothing were to come of it. Intellectual culture 'is the best aid to professional and scientific study ... ' for

> the man who has learned to think and to reason and to compare
> and to discriminate and to analyse, who has refined his taste, and
> formed his judgment, and sharpened his mental vision, will not
> indeed at once be a lawyer ... or an orator, or a statesman, or a
> physician, or a good landlord, or a man of business, or a soldier, or
> an engineer, or a chemist, or a geologist, or an antiquarian, but he
> will be placed in that state of intellect in which he can take up any
> one of the sciences or callings I have referred to ... with an ease, a
> grace, a versatility, and a success, to which another is a stranger. [12]

Here Newman does not argue (though I do not think he goes against
it) that any study that can be engaged in as a piece of liberal education
is a preparation for work in the professional schools; he is rather suggest-
ing that a particular group of subjects, literary, historical, philosophical,
and scientific, is a desirable preparation for this work. (This assumption
lay behind the practice of the *lycée* and the *Gymnasium*, in their upper
forms, in many European countries; it was not thought strange that a
student who intended to be a physicist or an architect should still be
studying classical and vernacular literature at a good level in the highest
forms or that one who intended to be a classical scholar should occupy
himself with the Calculus or Set Theory. I suspect things may be changing now.)

In the ninth Discourse ('Duties of the Church towards Knowledge')
Newman shows most clearly what he has in mind by commending what
might today be called 'a core curriculum.' Here he goes out of his ordinary way to affirm that natural science as well as literature is a part of
this core: 'the book of Nature is called Science, the book of man is called
Literature. Literature and Science, thus considered, nearly constitute
the subject-matter of Liberal Education.' [13] We may set aside what he has
to say about Natural Science, for Newman is here an amateur, though a

well-informed one. (It is characteristic of Newman's acuteness in scientific matters that at the end of 1863, four years after the appearance of *The Origin of Species*, he wrote in a private notebook that he was prepared to 'go the whole hog with Darwin.')[14]

'Literature stands related to Man as Science stands to Nature; it is his history.'[15] Again: 'Literature is to man in some sort what autobiography is to the individual; it is his Life and Remains.'[16] As we have already seen, if there is anything in the common talk today about our passing through a crisis of identity, or quiddity, one remedy is to study literature, not simply for the sake of those texts that give us aesthetic pleasure, but also for the reasons here given by Newman, that literature, and within it the oral traditions we only know about because they have come to be written down, is our history, our life-story. As such, it is irreplaceable. Teachers of philosophy often discover that what is able to give weight and seriousness to philosophical discussion is a work of literature. Death is a topic that even philosophers of an austere kind can scarcely avoid. What can be more useful, not simply as an apt story, a parable, but as an account of one man's death that is for the attentive reader a source of self-knowledge – of course, not in an easy moralistic sense – than Tolstoy's short story *The Death of Ivan Illyich*? And if we are to concern ourselves with evil, dense, purblind, dark evil, in human affairs, what is more relevant than *Lear*? or the great fairy story in the Grimms' collection, *The Juniper Tree*? If we are to reflect upon the perplexities of moral and civic duty, what is more sustaining than the *Antigone* of Sophocles? And yet in all these cases we are entering worlds that are in many senses immensely remote from us.

For Newman, as for almost all his contemporaries, even those formed by the creed of Utility, literature meant in the first place the textual and historical study of the surviving writings of the ancient Greeks and Romans. Even for a Christian, Athens was, along with Jerusalem, a *patria*, a second home or native country. So it had been among Christians from the moment when Tertullian's anguished: *What has Athens to do with Jerusalem? What has the Academy to do with the Church?* was no longer needed. The clerks are reading Horace and Catullus in the darkness of the ninth century. The young men who in the twelfth century swarmed into Paris to hear the great Abelard lecture were primarily concerned with letters; and their songs and poetry, fresh and original and very unlike the Latin verse of the classical period, is all the same nourished by the Roman lyrical poets.[17] Their work is an influence in the making of the great vernacular literatures that flower in Provence and Tuscany and, in England, with Langland and Chaucer, and then later with Ronsard and du Bellay and the English lyric writers of the sixteenth century. It becomes plain to us, if not always to our grandfathers, for whom the battle of the Ancients and the Moderns still reverberates a little, that a new classical culture was being achieved in Europe, at least from the moment when Dante's *Divina Commedia* appears. If men go on mulling over the literary remains of antiquity, it is because in a superficial sense the writers in the European vernaculars derive their material from the old writers. To read Shakespeare and Milton with understanding we need at least to have a classical dictionary to hand. But it is also plain, and Newman, with his proposal for a chair of English literature at the new university in Dublin, saw this, that the vernacular literatures are classics in their own right. His position is set out in the three lectures, 'Christianity and Letters,' 'Literature,' and 'English Catholic Literature.'

With many of his contemporaries he continued to believe that as far into the future as men could look the study of Latin and Greek literature would go on in the grammar schools; and that, therefore, all those who would enter the university, to study whatever subject, would have at least some acquaintance with the problems of syntax and style as these came up in translations and proses and verse compositions, and would have some rudimentary knowledge of Greek and Roman history and mythology. There was, he thought, simply no substitute for this kind of education, even though he believed that in principle studying the classics of the modern European vernaculars – Shakespeare, Milton, Molière, Racine – could be the staple of a liberal education. We now see that his view of the future was mistaken; and we need not go into the multitude of reasons for the decline of classical studies, the disappearance even among classical scholars of any strong belief that the Greek and Latin classics are uniquely fitted to provide the staple of a liberal education. The fact is enough for us. It is even possible to hear in universities where the ancient languages have not been abandoned murmurings to the effect that in times of economic stress it would be well to dispense with Greek and perhaps with Latin. The impious nature of such proposals is evident, but it would not be altogether astonishing if here and there they were to be acted upon.

One reason for Newman's confidence in the future of classical studies was his view that European civilization, that civilization and culture which grew up round the Mediterranean, with its sources in Greece and Egypt and Mesopotamia and North Africa and Italy, is roughly equivalent to *human* civilization. His confidence does not rest upon his Christian belief, though he allows that the interpenetration of Christianity and classical culture is a precious element of this civilization. One gets the impression from what he writes that he thinks European civilization would have been, uniquely, human civilization even without Christianity. It is at this point we feel remote from Newman, for we lack, from all kinds of causes and for many reasons good and bad, the enormous self-confidence of an Englishman of the Victorian age. I deliberately say *Englishman;* for I am inclined to think other Europeans would have been less positive. Ever since the despatches from China of the first Jesuits there, in the seventeenth century, had startled Europe, ever since the great Jesuit Nobili had sought to become a Brahmin and enter Hindu society, confidence in the identification of European with human civilization had been shaken.[18] Perhaps we ought to let Newman have his say.

> Considering, then, the characteristics of this great civilized society ... I think it has a claim to be considered as the representative Society and Civilization of the human race, as its perfect result and limit, in fact; – those portions of the race which do not coalesce with it being left to stand by themselves as anomalies, unaccountable indeed, but for that very reason not interfering with what on the contrary has been turned to account, and has grown into a whole. I call then this commonwealth pre-eminently and emphatically Human Society, and its intellect the Human Mind, and its decisions the sense of mankind, and its disciplined and cultivated state Civilization in the abstract, and the territory on which it lies the *orbis terrarum*, or the World.[19]

The argument is that European civilization and culture are normative, that they set standards that are final and definitive of what is human in the highest possible degree. I think we have to say that for us such a view is quite out of the question. This scarcely needs to be argued. Our view of a civilization and culture has to be empirical, not normative; and I think that Christians in particular have to be clear that this is so. In so far as Christianity has remained the creature of European culture in its linguistic and institutional forms, it has limited its own inner movement towards the universal, the truly human. (I would not argue that the truly human stands above and outside all particular cultures, but that all human cultures are, as Ranke said of historical periods, equally near to – or far from – God.) It is possible to see the defeat of the Jesuits on the question of the Chinese Rites, and the defeat of those Jesuits who wanted to root Christianity in Hindu culture, as great blunders of history. Had they been avoided it seems possible, though of course not likely, the history of the world would have taken a different turn.

Newman seems clearly wrong in taking European civilization and culture to constitute the human world (he has an extraordinary statement about the civilization of China: 'it is a huge, stationary, unattractive, morose civilization');[20] but there is indeed one sense in which we have to consider European civilization unique, and it is this which has made it in fact, at least in its present development (or decadence), the civilization of the planet. It is the civilization within which industrial capitalism and all that has come of it was engendered and deployed; and it is precisely within this latest development of a world civilization European in its style that the great achievements of the mind represented by those subjects that make up liberal studies have come under attack, or have come to be despised and neglected. Such achievements had persuaded Newman to believe, innocently and not without generosity of spirit, that European civilization was normative for mankind. The mistake sprang from an affection for what deserved it. It is not a mistake he would have repeated had *per impossibile* his life-span been doubled.

Nevertheless, the works of intellect, imagination, organizing ability, from Justinian to the Common Law, from Homer to Henry James, from the Greek *polis* to constitutional parliamentary government, all these are our gift to the world; this is the matrix out of which we have come. No matter how much it may come to be changed and enriched by other cultures it will remain for as long as need concern us the culture we have to re-live and appropriate if we are to understand ourselves. We are what the seven liberal arts* have made us, and if we were to forget them we should be undone. We should be like men who had forgotten their names and where they were born. Literature is the only channel through which the oral culture of earlier ages, no doubt much transformed but still a source of life, comes to us; with the decay of liberal education this unique means of self-knowledge would be lost.

* Grammar, Rhetoric, Dialectic, Music, Arithmetic, Geometry, Astronomy.

II

Colleges
Universities
and the State

At the beginning of his great work on the history of the medieval university Rashdall notes that for one writer of that time there were 'three mysterious powers or "virtues," by whose harmonious co-operation the life and health of Christendom are sustained.'[1] These three powers are *Sacerdotium, Imperium, Studium*; or, as we should say, Church, State, University. The reputed power of the university lasted until at least the end of the Middle Ages. Henry VIII thought it worth while to canvas Oxford and Cambridge in the great matter of his divorce suit against Catherine his Queen. The opinion of the University of Salamanca was asked for by the Spanish Crown in the matter of the conquest of the Americas: Was it or was it not lawful to conquer and bear rule over the American Indians? 'I love the University of Salamancha [said Doctor Johnson]; for when the Spaniards were in doubt as to the lawfulness of their conquering America, the University of Salamancha gave it as their opinion that it was not lawful.'[2] It is true that in these particular cases *Imperium* was interested in getting only one kind of answer from *Studium*, and *Sacerdotium* looked the other way; but there is an implied recognition of the university's virtue in that its opinion was asked at all. Universities (more often, perhaps, university departments) are today often consulted on technical matters, about the pollution of the air or water, or the design of weapons, or problems of statistical analysis; but it is rare for them to be consulted on important moral and political issues – though on such matters professorial advice is rarely stinted – and their advice on crucial moral and political decisions is rarely, so far as I know, solicited. Perhaps it should be noted, as slightly mitigating my bald statement, that in a neighbouring State it is the custom for the head of the Executive to raid the sacred groves and to carry off some of the denizens, very willing captives, to serve the *Imperium*. Despite such an example, in general the notion that the *Studium*, still more the *Sacerdotium*, should be treated as a competent advisor in such matters would be thought against the democratic principle.

The universities, then, are not in the modern world taken to be corporate moral powers. From time to time they may in fact strive after such a role, and from time to time and from place to place, where men are resisting tyrannies, or where an issue of policy divides the nation (as in the United States during the Vietnam War), the universities may show some inclination to be the moral mentors of their society; and the capitulation of the university before wicked rulers is, like the capitulation of the *Sacerdotium*, something terrible, from which a society recovers slowly and with difficulty. That we should continue to expect much of universities, that we should be greatly disappointed when they fail to be heroic or even dignified, these things suggest that despite our commitment to formal democracy ('every man to count for one and no man to count for more than one') we do in times of distress seek to call up the mighty ghost of the medieval *Studium*, the power or virtue of a corporation consecrated to learning and dialectic.

That university which is, as Rashdall says, 'distinctly a medieval institution – as much so as constitutional kingship, or parliaments, or trial by jury,'[3] was an invention of the late twelfth and early thirteenth centuries, and since this invention was to have as long a career as the other medieval institutions mentioned, and was to penetrate regions where neither constitutional government nor trial by jury has ever flourished, it may be useful to ask if there are any peculiar features we may think without extravagance to belong to the essence of the institution.

There seem to be two such features: first, the university is a *studium generale;* then, it is an *universitas*. Neither term has at the beginning any suggestion of what later comes to be attached to each. Newman, though he knows this is not historically accurate, thinks usage has decided that a university 'is a place of teaching universal knowledge,'[4] a place in which the full circle of the arts and sciences, so far as they can be studied liberally, is taught and professed. No doubt, even for Newman, this is an ideal development, not a state of affairs ever to be found in practice. But *studium generale* means in its beginning 'a place where students from all parts are received,'[5] that is, an institution of higher learning, if it is to be a *studium generale*, is an ecumenical institution, a place of general resort for students from the entire civilized world; and the existence, often troubled and tumultuous, of the many 'nations' living side by side in the European universities of the Middle Ages, vividly illustrates this. Freedom to study where one may choose, and freedom, provided one is a Master, to offer one's services as a teacher in any European university, these are the earliest academic freedoms. This is to say that such is the ethos required by the principles of the medieval university. In practice, it seems that the great pioneering universities, Paris, for example, and Bologna, were wary of accepting teachers whose degrees had been conferred by newer foundations. It is stupefying, at least to some of us, to discover that 'at Paris, even Oxford degrees failed to command incorporation without fresh examination and licence, and Oxford repaid the compliment by refusing admission to Parisian doctors'[6] – and all this in defiance of a papal Bull forbidding such discrimination. All the same, we are in this early period of university history far from that deformation of the original idea that was to follow the coming of nation states and the triumph of the vernacular cultures.

Universitas is a term that was only after some time identified with the *studia generalia* or with academic institutions at all. *Universitates* were originally mere guilds or clubs of masters or undergraduate students. They began to serve as adjuncts of the *studium generale*, first in Paris and Bologna, and later, by migration or infection, in other universities, until in the end it was normal for the affairs of the *studium generale* to be largely conducted by the *universitas* of masters, or of students, or by some arrangement between the two. The derived term 'university' means, then, the self-government of students, or masters, or both, in the conduct of the affairs of the *studium generale*.

The university is in its formative period a place of general resort for those who want to know and to teach, and it is, within the limits imposed by Church and State, a corporation which manages its own affairs. Of the development of colleges within the university I will give some account later.

The history of the university since the twelfth century is too vast a field, and too complex, for me to attempt even the most sketchy account of it. The shifts and transitions that lead from Abelard's lecturing at Ste Geneviève down to Chomsky's lecturing at MIT or Frye's and McLuhan's lecturing at the University of Toronto are too multitudinous; no comprehensive account of them could be given. But some characteristics are obvious if not always well-known and may be picked out even by the casual student.

There is the *vitality* of the institution, under all kinds of regimes and through many vicissitudes and even what were taken to be mortal illnesses. Nothing could be more acridly amusing and nothing could be sadder than eighteenth-century Oxford: meaningless exercises in place of serious examinations; idle and drunken tutors and idle and drunken undergraduates; odious class distinctions, marked by dress and habits of life, between undergraduates; the frequent profanation of services in the college chapels. Lord Chancellor Eldon took his Bachelor's degree in the Hilary Term of 1770. An examination, he used to say, 'was a farce in my time. I was examined in Hebrew and in History. "What is the Hebrew for a place of a skull?" I replied, Golgotha. "Who founded University College?" I stated (though by the way the point is sometimes doubted) that King Alfred founded it, "Very well, sir," said the examiner, "you are competent for your degree." '[7] Generalizations must be used with caution, though, for there were then some worthy scholars in the ancient universities. Martin Routh (who advised the young Burgon always to verify his references[8]), the President of Magdalen who died in his hundredth year, who remembered Doctor Johnson as an undergraduate, and to whom Newman in 1838 dedicated his *Lectures on the Prophetical Office of the Church*, was a fine patristic scholar. The mathematical tradition of the great Newton persisted at Cambridge. But the general picture is one of standards of learning and conduct that have fallen far below the level of mediocrity. And yet nineteenth-century Oxford is remarkable for its originality, scholarly industry, and strong feeling of responsibility for the teaching of undergraduates, and the ascent from the eighteenth-century depths is begun well before the reform of 1854. As places of scholarly inquiry and speculative boldness neither of the ancient English universities may be compared with the German universities of that period, though they had perhaps more sense of the needs of undergraduate education. All the same, the recovery is there to see, and it is at least in part self-generated. This ability of universities to generate their own restored life is what I mean by vitality.

What was true then of Oxford and Cambridge was true at an earlier period of the Scottish universities in the time of David Hume and Adam Smith. And I need not speak of the German universities of the period or of the extraordinary re-founding of the University of Paris after the Revolution, of the brilliant successes of institutions of a new kind – though they manifestly are of the university type – such institutions as the Ecole Polytechnique, the Ecole Normale Supérieure, and others, or of the growth of the university in the United States, from its modest beginnings at Harvard and Yale and Charlottesville, Virginia, to the luxuriant growth of the twentieth century. All the books tell these stories in detail. Here, I simply pick out the plain evidence of the persistence and ingenuity of institutions that combine, with whatever accidental imperfections, the two fundamental characteristics of the medieval university: the *studium generale* and the *universitas*. They are self-governing institutions and places of general resort for the cultivation of liberal studies, and they meet the practical needs of their societies through the study of the natural sciences, of medicine, of some of the technologies, and of law. Even in the most unfavourable circumstances, as for example in totalitarian societies, the assembling of masters and pupils seems to generate a desire for independence and a critical spirit, a hatred of narrow nationalism, an interest in the whole world of learning. So it is that in a world in which monarchy is a cultural fossil, the Holy Roman Empire not even an influential ghost, in which the free movement of persons from country to country is scrutinized with anxious care even by liberal societies, the *studium generale* and the *universitas* persist.

It would not be seemly to display the universities of the civilized world as more excellent than they are. They share the characters of the societies in which they work and from which they draw their daily bread. Many administrators, teachers, and students within them may be venal and nationalistic, muddled by sophistries, devoted in part to studies that are unworthy of a university and perhaps of any educational institution, narrow, pedantic, worldly, full of intrigue and given to the petty politics of a small society, half-hearted in the defence of those standards that alone justify their leisured existence. The university is as much in need of continual reform as the Church. But all this is just to say that universities are human societies. It would be a sign of immaturity and lack of experience to expect the university community to be altogether different in such respects from the rest of society; and university teachers and scholars are as much subject to professional deformations as schoolmasters, clergymen, and lawyers. But anyone who has worked in the university for thirty or forty years or so will remember teachers and scholars who seemed to concentrate in their persons the virtue of the university. I remember the gentle majesty of R.H. Tawney, the splenetic and volcanic genius of R.G. Collingwood, the synoptic mind of Etienne Gilson (always to be mentioned with honour in the University of Toronto and especially in Saint Michael's College), and a few others, men and women who gave flesh and therefore argumentative weight to the great commonplaces of Newman and of all those who have written so captivatingly about the university. They are reminders in dark moments that this sacred institution has indeed been visited by the Muses, if it is not a place of their perpetual inhabitation, that at times the university ideal could be incarnated, could speak to the world in and through the bodily existence of men who could smoke their pipes and fall asleep after dinner like any one of the rest of us. But such a scholar is unlike the rest of us: he is, as Newman was, in Newman's great phrase (though not used by him of himself), 'master of the two-fold Logos, the thought and the word, distinct, but inseparable from each other.'[9] It is true, in using these words Newman has in mind the great imaginative writer (he gives Shakespeare as an instance of such mastership); but it can be the case, and is so in the cases of Tawney and Collingwood and Gilson, as it was in an earlier generation with Maitland and Peirce and William James, that historians and philosophers and critics show us this mastery.

The *studium generale* with the *universitas*, then, the place which is a general resort of scholarly men and the institution which is responsible for the conduct of its own life of study and teaching, is able to give itself new life, to be born again, even under very harsh conditions. It was born in a world of priests, nobles, peasants, craftsmen, citizens of places that were centres of a modest trade, of handicrafts, and of ecclesiastical administration; it was a poor world by present standards of opulence, a world full of bodily pain and foul diseases, a world fought over with barbarity by the *Sacerdotium* and the *Imperium* (or *Regnum*), a struggle I once felt moved, in a poem, to liken to the encounter of a serpent and a crocodile,

> ... the serpent and the crocodile
> twinned, twined in fire and sullen night.[10]

In such a world, the amount of the wealth of society given to the universities must have been immense; one hardly knows how the economies of Ireland and Sicily and Bohemia and Scotland could have spared the many young men who went off to Oxford or Paris or Bologna or Cologne, often enchanted at first by the music of dialectic, though no doubt a great many forgot the music and stayed to study law, canon and civil, the great path to advancement in such a society. At any rate, the young men must have devoured a great deal of society's modest surplus.

We are now concerned with the university in the last quarter of the twentieth century. What is its function in the opulent societies of western Europe, north America, and such other places – Australia and New

Zealand and perhaps Japan – as are by affiliation, and by similarity of social, economic, and political structure, in effect a part of what is called *western* society? I am not concerned directly with the universities of the Soviet Union and eastern Europe, and certainly not with the universities of the 'third' world, though their history and problems are of great interest and importance. Even though the universities of the Soviet Union, for instance, may be, in the intention of the Government, agents of the totalitarian regime, the very congregation of scholars and pupils in one place and within a single institution constitutes, as I have already suggested, a point of criticism and disaffection. In coming to this discussion we are necessarily concerned with principles of a very general character and with generalizations of a kind properly suspect in the view of historians and students of contemporary society. Mark Pattison remarked: 'life is made up of details; one cannot always be chewing the cud of great principles.'[11] But it is sometimes a good thing for teachers and administrators, immersed as they are in the research and teaching and overseeing of the university, to isolate general principles and to trace changes in the anatomy and metabolism of the university. There is no harm in this provided the principles, generalizations, hypotheses, are sufficiently salted with irony.

We have first to note that even in the most liberal societies, that is, in those societies in which, in matters of economic and social policy, the principle of *laissez faire* is given at least an occasional nod of respect, the relation between the university and the State (I assume that it is correct to say that provincial governments in Canada, state governments in the United States, are in fact parts of or organs of the State) is now coming to be almost as direct as the relation between the university and the State in the Germany of the nineteenth century and in France since Napoleon. This is merely a coming to be, a tendency, and tendencies can always be reversed. University teachers in Canada, the United States, and Great Britain are not yet civil servants, though they are sometimes seen as civil servants by members of the public; and it is also clear that in these universities, many of them private and local and (in Great Britain) having a very long history, are still in practice independent societies, however much they may be endowed or afflicted with governing bodies that represent the political authorities and other powers in society. But so many of their costs are met by the State, through direct subsidy, or through *ad hoc* grants for particular projects, or through grants and loans to students, that if the State fails to call the tune after paying the piper so handsomely this can only be because the weight of tradition inhibits the statesmen. English universities were for long the envy of the western world, for it was thought an ideal solution to the problem of how to pay for the universities without interfering with their freedom had been worked out. Government subsidies were allocated by a body, almost entirely composed of faculty members drawn from the various universities, called the University Grants Committee. Guidance and advice were offered, but no positive direction backed by sanctions was given. Further, it was generally and reasonably believed that the Grants Committee would always in periods of difficulty shield the universities from officious interference by the State. The position of the Committee has shifted in the past ten years or so and this shift is, given the economic situation, perfectly understandable. Something close to direction is now much more common and universities are often told what they may or may not do with their money.

The change in the policy of the Committee may be dated from a small incident, trivial and indeed ludicrous in itself, but nevertheless a sign of the coarsening of the sensibility and the decline in intellectual standards that are fairly general throughout the university world. In the academic year 1965–66 the Committee decided, no doubt in order to defend the universities against ill-informed criticism and to justify the amount spent on them, to ask the universities to find out from their senior members how their work was divided between preparation for undergraduate teaching, preparation for graduate teaching, and research. This inquiry was a logical absurdity, as any faculty member who does all three things can perceive. As a writer in *The* London *Times* put it, this is rather like interrogating a sheep as to how much of its time is devoted to growing wool and how much to turning itself into mutton. A university teacher related the following story. He was on holiday in Europe and went to see the performance of a classic play. He wrote an article about the play, lectured about it later to his undergraduate pupils, and still later founded a piece of published research on it. How was he supposed to reply to the questionary put out by the universities at the prompting of the Grants Committee? What was and is, even in retrospect, disturbing about this silly episode is that not one of the distinguished professors who were members of the Committee resigned over this issue and that not one university refused to take part in the exercise. The excuse offered in private was that the whole thing was so absurd that it was excessive to make a fuss over what was so plainly self-defeating. How terrible it is that learned bodies should go through what they all the time took to be a solemn pantomime! Alas, it seems altogether possible that the spurious statistics generated by this inquiry were later used as guides for policy. Some departments* in some universities refused to submit any returns. This was ill received by university administrations and I think it quite likely that some kind of return was made on behalf of the recalcitrants. This episode discloses an acceptance of unreality and it is thus a dark sign of worse things to come.

Perhaps the felt necessity to be on terms of great friendship and deep understanding with the political authorities is bound to generate humbug. The real business of the university and the conditions under which it is best pursued are not easy to explain to a public that stands outside the university world. Things may be thought to happen for the best when those who hold political power are themselves reflective about their own educational experiences and are prepared, if they are convinced they ought to, to stand by the interests of the universities without falling into the debased rhetoric that goes with much public talk about education. This rhetoric takes the form not so much of nonsense as of what I can only call *para-sense*. It sounds like sense: words, phrases, clauses, are gummed together to form what are grammatically speaking sentences. But since such pieces of discourse are filled with words and expressions that in their typical uses have neither sense nor reference – there is talk of 'open-ended situations,' 'meaningful relations,' 'catalysts' (where no catalysts, no matter how metaphorical, can be), problems which have 'parameters,' and the rest of the jargon that makes so much

---

* I am proud to say my own department at Leeds was one of these.

talk about education so painful, so idiotic – it is all as parasensical as the first verse of Lewis Carroll's *Jabberwocky*, as parasensical but not as amusing. Parasensical discourse is not likely to provoke public criticism, for the public, and here the universities may be blamed, has been persuaded that matters of deep import have to be talked about in this mystifying way. We have here something like religious discourse of the kind that speaks of astral bodies, etheric vibrations, consciousness-raising, and uses such discourse to persuade us that conversation is good for our plants and that we do everything better under pyramidical structures.

Before I leave (for the moment) the topic of parasense I should like to emphasize that though parasensical discourse may lack sense and reference it is not without important functions; it is, curiously, a very effective means of communication, a means of communicating attitudes. Most of those who attend with interest to parasensical discourse, and even some of those who use such discourse, are its dupes. They conceive that something is being communicated, something difficult and important and as such demanding a special vocabulary. If the user of this vocabulary seems expert in it, the dupes among his listeners may be captured by feelings of reverential awe, in part before the speaker, in part before the sacred language. Hence, there is in the world of education a reverential attitude towards quite spurious authorities who are either the dupes of their own texts or conscious manipulators of parasensical discourse. One of the worst consequences of the vogue of parasense is that quite sensible people are overcome with anxieties that are put to sleep by parasensical locutions. A lady in public life complained recently that the members of the organization of which she is president did not talk to her; but she put her complaint in the form of the question: 'Why don't they come and give me input?' Again, I find in a recent issue of a religious periodical: 'The Canadian Religious Conference of Ontario held a weekend of consciousness – raising on social justice.' In these trivial cases no one is deceived. The lady who solicits 'input' plainly wishes to say (but seems to find it too crude): 'Why don't they come and talk to me?' The Conference of Religious spent a no doubt profitable weekend talking and thinking about social justice. But the connotations of 'input' and its giving, of 'consciousness-raising,' are those of esoteric spiritual operations worthy of this dignified nomenclature. Such are some of the corruptions for which education may be blamed.

The State is the custodian of the common interests of society (I speak of its function, not of its performance in this or that case) and it has therefore responsibilities of a serious kind for what goes on in education. Society has a concern in seeing to it that men and women grow up literate and able to do simple calculations, able to read a map, distinguish between north and south, right and left, have some rudimentary knowledge of natural science and of mechanical principles, some awareness of their historical past, and some acquaintance with the canon of literary and other artistic works that represent the achievement of their culture. It has also been thought that the State has obligations to safeguard the common religion of society, where it has one, and to cherish and further the moral development of the young. Certainly, society has often asked this of the State, though, for good historical reasons, we are wary of any regime that professes to be deeply concerned with the protection of religion and morality.

If the educated population can read and write only with difficulty, finds a map as strange as a medieval charter, does not know what the stars are but thinks their positions have something to do with the fortunes of men, cannot get in the right historical order (I do not say *date*) the American Revolution, the French Revolution, and the Reformation, is unacquainted with anything by Shakespeare, with the Bible, with the fairy stories of the brothers Grimm, with *The Pilgrim's Progress*, with some of the novels of the great nineteenth century, thinks Rockwell Kent a better painter than Matisse (a maker of childish daubs), then we are disposed to think the State ought to have ordered matters differently. If the image of bright success for the young man – there would presumably be a corresponding image for the young woman – is that of a well-barbered and sharply dressed lout who steps out of his Mercedes or Porsche, a copy of *Penthouse* or *Playboy* under his arm and an American Express card in his pocket, and strolls through the doors of an expensive hotel to sexual and business success, then we are inclined to feel that the State or the schools or the universities have in some way let us down.

We may also speak darkly of the breakdown of family discipline, the ineffectiveness of the churches, the dire influence of the culture of the United States, and other favoured topics. In such matters each of us considers himself as wise as Solomon or Aristotle. We are in fact terrified, for we find ourselves in a world lying beyond our control, a world we cannot force to meet our expectations. Clearly, we do not understand the dynamics of cultural change; and since we are encouraged to think of society as something that, like the world of inanimate nature, would be malleable if we knew the facts and had the right hypotheses, we think that somewhere there must be bodies of men able to understand and to control and to bring about the good life; and that it is the business of the State, having under its hand the potent engine of education, to present us with a satisfactory plan of action.

There are no such hypotheses, there are no such bodies of men. To entertain such expectations of the State and of its bureaucratic instruments is dangerous, for it relieves us of those responsibilities, small and not so small, that can be undertaken by individual men and by small groups, and it may also breed delusions of grandeur in statesmen who may conceive vast and vain ambitions. In matters of culture generally, in the matter of education in particular, we have to go forward taking short steps, feeling our way with caution and relying on our memory of those measures that have in the past turned out to be profitable. It is a great thing to live in a *Rechtsstaat*, in a political society subject to the rule of law and to the obstructive force of convention. Within the web of what often seem to be frustrating laws and conventions we are given time for reflection. Where the all-wise party is not faced with the obstructive force of law and convention, entire generations may be sacrificed to social plans for which there is not one scrap of empirical justification. The decision by the Soviet Government to collectivize agriculture is perhaps the most spectacular instance. Not only did millions perish as a consequence of this foolish decision; Soviet agriculture is even today poor and crippled; a country that can put men into space and design intercontinental missiles is unable, despite its having abundant natural resources, to feed itself. The partially successful attempt of successive British Governments to destroy the ancient grammar schools of England or drive them out of the public system is a melancholy instance of what may turn out to be a catastrophe for secondary education in that country.

In what I have to say about the State's role in education I want to make a distinction that is perhaps a fine one. We may think of transforming and reshaping the educational system through the enlightened policy of the State. Reformers often believe that a combination of enlightenment and power at the centre of the political system will transform education and, through the transformed education, make everyone happier and better. This is the view of vulgar Marxists and of some highminded liberals and social democrats. There is not a scrap of evidence in support of such views. Nevertheless, since the State ought to be concerned with the common interests of society, and since in a free society no government is likely to last long which grossly flouts these interests, we are bound to grant the State a role in the formation of education at every level. Indeed, there is some historical evidence to suggest that without the gentle pressure of the State, universities that have fallen into bad ways are unlikely to reform themselves. But it is best if they reform themselves. Reconstructing a university and doing it under the command of those who stand outside the university is necessarily a painful process; it checks precisely those energies that are needed for the reconstruction of the university *as* a university, that is, as a corporation that runs its own affairs. We cannot in the last resort deny the right and duty of the State to intervene directly in education, when things are plainly going very badly in the schools and universities. If it really were true that the public schools were, through their own incompetence, failing to give boys and girls the basic information and the basic skills they need to get through life without too much vexation, we should surely expect the State on our behalf to look at the curriculum, at the practices of teaching, and at the education in the universities of those who are to be teachers later on, to look into all this and to make proposals for change. It seems to me a possible thing (I have Great Britain in mind rather than Canada, though I dare say Canadian institutions are also in question) that a Government should appoint a committee to look into what goes on in Schools and Institutes of Education, and to make recommendations for reform. Public authority has often, directly or indirectly, woken the schools and universities out of their dogmatic slumbers.

All the same, a university is a *studium generale* and an *universitas*. Governments will always fail to do full justice to the ecumenical character of the university, will be too sensitive to the complaints of narrow nationalists who want to know why their taxes should support foreign students or why foreigners should be preferred to their own nationals for university posts. (Canadian universities are so much more generous in this respect than most others that this point does not perhaps need a great deal of emphasis here and now. But Canada, a centre of English and French culture, is so wonderfully and providentially – if one may say this – fitted to give a good example of the ecumenical spirit in university matters, that one trembles lest it, too, should be subdued by the grosser superstitions of the age.) They may also be impatient, and here again they will be responding to powerful populist sentiment, with the university's anxiety over interference from outside, with its resistance to attacks upon such institutions as tenured appointments. It is hard to explain why it is in the interest of the university, and in the long run in the interest of the society that nourishes the university and is nourished by it in return, that men and women who may seem unproductive scholars and poor teachers should nevertheless be kept in their posts until they retire or die. As Flexner once remarked, the conditions that permit idleness 'are [also] necessary to the highest exertion of human intelligence.'[12] Explanations of this can be given; but even when they are clear they will not necessarily be acceptable in a world where the conditions of employment are harsher and the employee can be more readily dismissed. This is why universities have a duty to see to it that their practices are defensible in ways that can be made plain to their critics. The independent existence of the university as a self-governing community of scholars, teachers, and students may rest upon our ability to explain, patiently and with good humour, what a university is and on what principles it is necessarily founded.

To speak of a university as independent and self-governing is not to say what kind of internal government it has – here the parallel with states is obvious. It may be tyrannical, oligarchic, resemble a Bonapartist regime (despotism tempered by plebiscite), or be a turbulent democracy, as are Oxford and Cambridge. To say of a university that it is independent is to say that it is independent of the political sovereign; to say that it is self-governing is to say that no body outside itself governs it. If it is tyrannical or oligarchic this may be a sign that its members are making a poor use of its independence; and such internal regimes may put the independence of the university in peril, either because there is little to stop a tyrant or a set of oligarchs bartering away the university's independence, or because tyranny and oligarchy are hateful to the rest of society. Some may want to argue that it makes no sense to speak of a corporate group that is genuinely independent of the sovereign authority. This may be a purely formal point of no great importance; but the point may be substantial. A brief response would be to say that within the countries of the Common Law it is not true that all persisting groups within society owe their legitimate authority to the political sovereign. Just as the rights of free speech and public assembly are prior to legislation by statute and indeed constitute the grammar by which legislation is construed, so the rights of such groups as churches, trade unions, universities, families, and the like to order their affairs within the law but independently of the State are also recognized. Here an old theme in political philosophy has some contemporary point.

We now turn to the question of colleges, that is, of collegiate bodies existing within the wider university. It is not easy to define colleges generically or by species. *College* is an umbrella term under which institutions of many kinds are to be found. In the medieval university the college was not a pastoral device for looking after the morals of the young men; at least, in its origins it had no pastoral intention. 'In the thirteenth century the Parisian arts-student of fourteen was, so far as the university was concerned, as free to live where and how he pleased as the canon or rector of twenty-five or thirty who had left his benefice in the country to read canon law at Paris or Bologna.'[13] We can discern a pastoral intention in the colleges of the religious orders, for these were naturally concerned with the spiritual condition of their members; but the other colleges were halls of residence, endowed by bishops, noblemen, wealthy citizens, and were designed to provide a roof, bed and board for particular groups of students. Setting aside the many colleges of the friars, about seventy colleges were founded in Paris before 1500.[14] At first it seems to have been well understood that students were to go outside their colleges for teaching in the university. But some teaching, ancillary at first to the university teaching, seems to have begun early in the colleges; and by the middle of the fifteenth century more education seems to have gone on within many of the colleges than outside them. In 1445 we find the University complaining formally to the king that 'almost the whole university resides in the colleges.'[15] This complaint is to be repeated by Newman five hundred years later.

With time the colleges of the European universities fell into decay and were extinguished. Only in England did colleges continue in vigour, both those founded in the Middle Ages and those founded on the same model after the Reformation. Indeed, to speak now of the collegiate system is to have in mind first of all the foundations, most though not all of them ancient, of Oxford and Cambridge. In their origins the various colleges are different and at one time their internal regimes varied a good deal; but with time their internal polities have become much the same. There is a body of fellows engaged in teaching, research and the management of the college's domestic and financial affairs (the great Keynes was the Bursar of King's College, Cambridge, and is said to have made it a very rich college indeed, though it appears there were some anxious moments on the road to opulence). There is a body of undergraduates, rarely more than three or four hundred even in a big college, a small number of graduate students, rare birds in my time but now a multiplying species; and over the whole college there reigns and sometimes rules a Master or a Provost or a Warden or a Principal or a President elected by the fellows. Many of the undergraduates in the bigger colleges will get most of their teaching from the tutorial fellows, though they will go to lectures (if they do) outside the college; for perhaps two years of their stay in the university they will live in college and will eat their dinners at the long tables in the great hall of the college. Common living and eating represent the origin of the college in considerations of convenience; if the college has continued to prosper it is because living a common life of sorts seems sensible and may even, at fortunate moments, be positively agreeable.

One condition of the continued existence and prosperity of the Ox-

ford and Cambridge colleges was that they were great owners of property, first in land and later in other kinds of wealth. That they had and
controlled their own income was a source of independence and, sometimes, a cause of sloth and luxury. The money was often used splendidly,
as anyone who has seen the buildings and examined the ancient libraries
of the Oxford and Cambridge colleges will agree; and if more was spent
on the kitchen and the cellar than was always judicious and consonant
with the life of learning – well, they were men of their time; and when
we remember the physical rigours of the age, it is hard to be censorious.

Economic independence conferred on the colleges a political independence of the university; and for long the tendency was for the colleges almost to extinguish the university. Newman thought the wealth
and power of the colleges a cause of the lack of intellectual distinction
in the Oxford of the early nineteenth century. He sees the occupant of
the professorial chair as representing the gathering of new knowledge
and new interpretations, the college as representing order and corporate
tradition; 'for though Professors may be and have been utterly without
personal weight and persuasiveness, and Colleges utterly forgetful of
moral and religious discipline, still, taking a broad view of history, we
shall find that Colleges are to be accounted the maintainers of order,
and Universities the origins of movement.'[16] The ideal university is here
seen as a polity in which powers and functions are separated; and it is
good that this separation, and the tension between the institutions em-
bodying them, should be.

A University embodies the principle of progress, and a College
that of stability; the one is the sail, and the other the ballast; each
is insufficient in itself for the pursuit, extension, and inculcation
of knowledge; each is useful to the other. A University is the scene
of enthusiasm, of pleasurable exertion, of brilliant display, of win-
ning influence, of diffusive and potent sympathy; and a College is
the scene of order, of obedience, of modest and persevering dili-
gence, of conscientious fulfilment of duty, of mutual private services, and deep and lasting attachments. The University is for the

world, and the College is for the nation. ... The University is for theology, law, and medicine, for natural history, for physical science ... ; the College is for the formation of character, intellectual and moral, for the cultivation of the mind, for the improvement of the individual, for the study of literature, for the classics, and those rudimental sciences which strengthen and sharpen the intellect.[17]

If Newman is right in his distinction of functions within the university (I am concerned with the way he distinguishes functions, not with his placing of the functions), then it would seem that we have in some way to provide for the two main groups of functions even within universities not at all organized in the way he takes for granted. But there is a further element in the collegiate system on which we are, I think, bound to attend to the evidence offered by Newman.

When the mind is most impressible, when the affections are warmest, when associations are made for life, when the character is most ingenuous and the sentiment of reverence is most powerful, the future landowner, or statesman, or lawyer, or clergyman comes up to a College in the Universities. There he forms friendships, there he spends his happiest days; and, whatever his career there, brilliant or obscure, virtuous or vicious, in after years, when he looks back on the past, he finds himself bound by ties of gratitude and regret to the memories of his College life. ... The routine of duties and observances, the preachings and the examinations and the lectures, the dresses and the ceremonies, the officials whom he feared, the buildings or gardens that he admired, rest upon his mind and his heart, and their shade becomes a sort of shrine to which he makes continual silent offerings of attachment and devotion. It is a second home, not so tender, but more noble and majestic and authoritative.[18]

Here the association with the college induces an attachment of the heart and an ordering of the affections. Towards the end of the *Apologia*

Newman shows us his own heart and pierces us when, as he describes his last leave-taking of Oxford, he tells us that he took leave of his first college, Trinity, in the person of his old tutor; and then recalls that 'there used to be much snap-dragon growing on the walls of my freshman's rooms there, and I had for years taken it as the emblem of my own perpetual residence even unto death in my University.'[19]

This is a vanished world. Our feelings about the university, the church, love and friendship, the authority of authorities – these cannot be what they were for Newman in his time, just as Newman's thoughts and feelings are for the most part quite unlike anything that would have been possible in the university of Scotus or Roger Bacon or Ockham. But the attachment of the heart to places and people is not as such something that belongs only to ancient places, to special historical moments. If I may speak personally: my Oxford memories are still affecting; but for me there is something even more affecting in the remembered sight of the mill chimneys and the spires, smoke-wreathed, in the folded hollows of the city, as one came upon them from Woodhouse Moor, and then descended a little to the splendid red-brick Gothic of the old Yorkshire College, the first cell of the great University of Leeds. And I dare say (to speak of Toronto) that to come upon the midnight silence of Queen's Park in the dead of winter may in youth touch the heart and remain, mingled with the sweetness and bitterness of youthful experience, for life.

The utility of the collegiate principle, then, seems to be that it provides an element of balance within the university. Even if, as must be the case (the experience of those modern English universities that have tried to set up colleges on something like the ancient model shows this), the economic and political conditions that enabled colleges to be great powers in the nation cannot be revived, there may be analogous institutional devices that will usefully diversify the internal structure of the university. To these matters I return later.

About the collegiate system in this University of Toronto I hesitate to speak, though plainly something has to be said. The system that prevailed when I first came to this country in 1971 has changed and will go on changing. It is perhaps worth noting that such changes are not the inevitable and irreversible processes they are often thought to be; their hypnotic power over the observer is immense, but we have to remember that they are still matters for decision and that earlier decisions can be revised. The federated colleges are powers in their own right and have the titles and the degree-granting powers of universities. The presence within the University of Saint Michael's College (to speak of the institution I know best) of two centres of graduate study, the Pontifical Institute of Mediaeval Studies and the Institute of Christian Thought, shows that the claim to the status of a university within the broader institution of the University of Toronto is not purely formal. The three Christian colleges represent different traditions that have come together in fraternity to pay their debts to higher education in the Province of Ontario. They represent, in my view, a happier answer to the question how to arrange the contribution of the churches to higher education than do the denominational colleges and universities in the United States.

Universities, then, independent of the State, but always linked with it and inevitably and rightly under its pressure, largely financed from public funds but not thereby required to furnish in return just what the community may from time to time happen to want, internally diversified through colleges and other devices for breaking down the larger institution into smaller, more intimate groups with their own degree of independence over against the university considered as a single power, such seem to be in rough outline the requirements, approved by good sense and our historical experience, for universities now. How far what seems desirable is in the darkness of our time possible is another question. The ironies of history are many. The university as multiversity was, by one of its princes, Dr Clark Kerr, the then President of the University of California, pronounced to be a happy mutation;[20] and this was on the eve of the explosion that half-paralyzed so many of the great American universities.

III

The Crisis of the University

'Crisis' is an immensely overworked term. It is often used to heighten interest in whatever subject-matter is being talked about. Seven or eight years ago 'crisis' would have meant 'unrest on the campus,' at least in talk about the university's affairs. I shall mean by crisis a moment at which the various forces and influences that make the character of the university are so related that the next stage in the development of the university is not irrevocably decided. I believe we have reached such a moment. What the university will be in ten or twenty or a hundred years does not depend upon forces that determine it to go in only one direction; we are not prisoners of a blind process of development. How strenuously we think about the present of the university, how far we grasp its central problems, whether or not we have the courage to act upon those proposals that seem the wisest after thought has done all it can, these are matters within our power. What I offer here is not a grand solution to all the university's problems; it is an attempt, as honest and as well-thought-out as I can make it, to say how the present strikes one who is necessarily the prisoner of his own time and experiences. We are all in this position. There are no plausible educational saviours who, like the terrible political saviours of our time, have a single liberating doctrine. All we can hope to assemble is some knowledge of our history, some experience of men and affairs, some feeling for the wisdom to be found in our own long intellectual tradition. With the best will and the best thought we may fail. Perhaps it is a mistake to fret too much over consequences. Christians above all ought not to be concerned about success, for they place themselves under the sign of a worldly failure as complete as failure can be.

The senior members of the university think of themselves as members of a proletariat. The undergraduates are estranged from the entire senior body, from their teachers, from the university administration. Great teachers and scholars who are short on bureaucratic skills evade the requirements of bureaucracy by ignoring circulars, requests for grades, the shower of acronyms and numbers that symbolizes the activity of administration; their secretaries and junior colleagues have to assume the burden. Graduate students fret over their comprehensive examinations and the choosing from a well-worked field of a thesis topic that will pass the PhD committee of their department, interest a supervisor, and get them a job in a chosen profession. Administrators feel themselves estranged from the teachers and scholars: they are misunderstood, their motives are thought to be bad, they are depicted as power-hungry, without heart, and they are the objects of professorial paranoia. On the fringes of the programmes of the faculties of arts and social science, traditionally minded senior members are disturbed to discover courses of a doubtful kind, or what appear to be such: Black studies, Gay studies, Women's studies, The Occult, Yoga, Astrology, UFO studies ... no matter how strange, how inappropriate for university study a subject may be, somewhere in North America you will find it snuggled up to the great body of the Multiversity. In all universities there has been a growth of medical and counselling services over the past twenty years, and a corresponding growth in the number of clients and in the conditions such services exist to cure; supply seems to generate demand. Those of us who have seen many things are still stupefied from time to time: to note for example that with the increase in the provision of information about contraceptives through university medical services and through other services off the campus, the number of abortion referrals seems to have increased. There are pin-ball machines rather than chessboards in the common rooms. We are tempted to emulate George Fox with his great cry: 'Woe, woe, to the bloody city of Lichfield!'

Such observations, complaints, judgments, are an indulgence in those morose pleasures that are among the consolations of the elderly, especially of those who pass unwillingly from activity to an enforced contemplation. None of them is ill-grounded; but if they altogether represented the truth about the universities in our day, these institutions would already have collapsed through inner decay. We have to remind ourselves that viewed from within and from without universities have always offered us rough scenes set in improbable landscapes. The great battle of 1354 fought in the streets of Oxford on St Scholastica's Day and the days following makes the turbulent affairs of the 'sixties seem rather small. Idleness, drunkenness, vicious horseplay and vandalism, low debauchery, narrowness, pedantry, complacency, poltroonery, these have characterized university life from the beginning. These or similar vices seem to belong necessarily to the congregation in one place of teachers of liberal studies and young men and women passing from adolescence to maturity. We may prefer the tranquillity of a well-ordered seminary, or the industrial discipline of a firmly directed factory. No doubt these are good institutions in their own way; but they are not universities; their kind of order is not a possible goal for those who wish to preserve or to construct a university.

All universities in all periods have been sustained and tolerated by the societies in which they have lived simply because there has been a general sense that their activities have produced men with the characters and accomplishments valued by society. If, over and above this, universities have also been centres where critical work, of a kind not immediately acceptable or intelligible to most men, has gone on, this has been tolerated, even defended, on account of the usefulness of universities. Modern universities in the United States illustrate this point as aptly as do the medieval universities. The presence of Chomsky at MIT or of Marcuse at the University of California or of defenders of a free market economy at the University of Chicago is not so much an example of genial toleration as of the value put upon the social functions of these universities. Men see, not always very clearly, that for work of the highest quality it is necessary to pay a high price: the toleration of social and political and intellectual eccentricity. Nevertheless, while there may be islands, even whole archipelagoes, of harsh dissent within universities, no university, unless it is financially self-sustaining, perhaps not even then, can itself be such an island. What there can be a doubt over is whether or not all that is now done by the university in the way of teaching, research and professional training, need be done by the university or is best done by the university. But that there are limits on what may be done in the way of change and reform, limits imposed by the pressures and demands of society, is certain, though one ought not to be too timid in deciding where the limits run. In giving an account, then, of the critical situation of the university, I do not wish to imply that there is available to us some utopian model of the university, one we could make actual, given good will or hard work or a bit of luck or the right kind of political revolution. Western industrial society is what it is; and while we may hope that what is vicious and trivial in its culture may be diminished and that economic practices harmful to men and dangerous to the planet Earth may be reformed or abandoned, there is much we simply have to live with. Individuals, and especially individuals within universities, can and should cry out over our stupidities and wickednesses, but they can scarcely expect to overcome the inertia of institutions in a short time. And where problems are complex and highly technical, a becoming modesty is perhaps desirable in professors.

I begin with a symptom of the crisis, what I referred to earlier as parasensical discourse. I distinguish parasense from nonsense and straight gibberish. That a given sentence is nonsensical is perceived only if we place it in a standard context. A philosopher once gave as an instance of nonsense: 'Quadruplicity drinks procrastination.' It is a good instance but not without the power suddenly to achieve sense in a special context. It was pointed out that, as a description of a four-power conference, it was apt. Sense is, as it were, expressed – squeezed out – from a text where the context is of a kind to exert the right kind of pressure. (There used to be labels on bottles that claimed that the oil in them was 'freshly expressed' from the liver of the cod; this shows the appositeness of the metaphor sleeping in the verb 'to express.') 'The cat sat on the mat and then he ate the mouse.' Few of us have difficulty over this. What about this? 'The parameters of the problem can only be fully evaluated by those who are able to relate to the educational process in a meaningful way and thus interface-wise implement a viable solution in the ongoing future.' This one I invented myself, and perhaps 'interface-wise' makes it a little too rich to be quite credible. But one would not really be surprised to find it in the reported proceedings of some institution concerned with the subject known as Education, or, alas, even in a university document. It is totally parasensical. It differs from what may be taken as nonsense, in that there are no category blunders and no obvious logical foul-ups. It seems grammatical; its words are for the most part to be found in the standard dictionaries; the syntax conforms to standard models and thus our habitual expectations are fulfilled; above all, it is as though it were coated with a special kind of grease – it slips down (or past) easily. It may even be redeemable in a curious way: as being in code. We could understand by it: 'Only teachers and their pupils know where the shoe pinches and only they have anything sensible to say on the problem.' This would leave us with the difficulty of deciding why so plain a statement should be uttered in this code. Commonly, though, such a piece of parasense is chosen because it generates intellectual fog and induces a reverential attitude in the reader. It is like the chanting of a *mantra* or spell, except that a *mantra* may make beautiful sense for one who understands the religious discourse within which it is uttered; whereas this sentence can only be redeemed if it is decoded in the way I have suggested, and if *this* is what redeems it one is left with the question why such a fancy code was chosen to express what can be put plainly.

The metropolitan country of parasense is undoubtedly the United States; but there is a great deal of it in the other English-speaking countries. I choose a fine Canadian example of parasense from the published draft of the Wright Report on post-secondary education in Ontario. In the Report parasense is certainly very often used as a code; and one may guess what is intended, though not said out loud, by the following.

> We must commit ourselves to inspire new hope, particularly in the young, for life in the future, for having the courage to discard the irrelevant and to look to our educational goals, and methods of implementing man-serving institutions in the context of the society goals.[1]

It is extraordinary that such trash should have been published under the imprint of the Queen's Printer.

One would have to be a virtuoso to be parasensical continuously. There are such examples; the publications of the Church of Scientology contain the best examples of continuous pure parasense I have so far come across in English. (I suspect parasense is harder to achieve in French.) In any case, parasense gets its most startling effects from its being set in the context of language that has sense; too much parasense might provoke attitudes of suspicion rather than reverence.

The decadence of the language of the educated is also shown in uses that are not strictly parasensical. Now, what I have to say about contemporary uses of English does not spring from a desire to keep the language just as it is at a given stage of its development, nor have I any interest in commending genteel usage. Plainly, usage is king; language is always changing so long as it is used in matters of ordinary life. A changing language may be, as the American vernacular has so often been, a register of new exercises of wit and intelligence and of experiences not before noted. It may also represent a blunting of the mind's sharpness and a dulling of the sensibility. No one would wish to restore, except as an exercise of wit, obsolete senses of *prevent* and *deprecate*. But there are changes in the existing language that can certainly be justified by an appeal to usage but to which there are rational objections. (There changes are often associated with the kind of discourse which is ornamented with parasense.)

There are new usages which stand in the way of our making those distinctions that can be made by the usages now vanishing. Two examples: *unpractical* and *impracticable* have been collapsed into one word *impractical;* this leads us into vagueness and guessing. Then, there is the use of *disinterested* to mean *uninterested* (this is parallel to the strange use of *momentarily*, strange, and terrifying, too, as in the pilot's 'We shall be momentarily airborne'). This is an indefensible change. One would wish to be able to compliment a judge on his disinterestedness; this might now be taken by many to be a not too subtle insult. A usage for which nothing at all can be said is the merging of *deprecate* and *depreciate.* 'Merging' is too polite: the apt term is *confusion.*

Then, there is the use of false or hollow rhetoric, often marked by mixed metaphor. Here are two recent examples worth citing. One writer referred to 'remote pre-history, whose roots are lost in the mists of time.' The other example was in a letter to the press by a lecturer in sociology at a polytechnic. He was replying to a letter by a Professor X on the South African situation and wrote: 'But the pious veneer of Prof. [X's] letter is mere window-dressing ... '; this was followed by something even more thought- and mirth-provoking: 'Prof. [X] has written a letter which fulfils all the requirements of a "red herring" '. To echo Churchill: some letter, some herring.

Perhaps we should put together with false or hollow rhetoric something that lies between this rhetoric and parasense, the rhetoric of congratulation, something that is part of the professional skills of drummers, Rotarian orators, and other pressers of the flesh. A practitioner would be one who, encountering a new group of people, would say, necessarily ahead of his experience: 'You are very very lovely people.' Such language surely has no place in a university, or in a religious community. But we find it in both these milieux, though it is perhaps worse among the religious. I found the following in a religious periodical. (It was contained in a report of the work of a Christian family centre.) 'The concrete direction of the centre has not yet been spelled out. However, a concerned and creative group is being called together for the new year to address this crucial area in (*sic*) our society.' This is in fact a mixture of parasense and the rhetoric of congratulation. Spelling out a concrete direction is plainly a parasensical operation. What is unbearable is the note of self-congratulation – imagine the Apostle Paul telling his colleagues and catechumens they were 'concerned and creative'! That it is possible to write on religious topics without going in for the rhetoric of congratulation (or any of the vicious rhetorics) is shown by Dorothy Day in the *Catholic Worker* and her example has powerfully influenced her colleagues on the paper.

Parasense; linguistic confusion; false or hollow rhetoric; the rhetoric of congratulation: these are unhappy modes in which to conduct the verbal transactions of a body of learned men and of pupils in the course of becoming learned. I have by no means exhausted the vicious modes and have been frugal in my choice of examples. That I have pointed to a serious disease of institutions of the English-speaking world no one who looks at the relevant material can doubt. That it is a phenomenon of decadence seems obvious; language of this kind could not have existed without censorious notice in the England of Newman and Huxley, Thomas Arnold and George Eliot. I doubt that this corruption of the language is simply a consequence of changes in the ways in which men live in the opulent industrial societies, though plainly it is in part a consequence of such changes. But that such rhetorical models should beguile men whose training in language and its skills would, one would have guessed, have protected them from corruption must be connected with changes within the university community itself. The world of the university has a kind of unreality; in addressing ourselves to the most serious intellectual and practical problems we find ourselves among shadows; problems are felt rather than stated, evaded rather than looked at, covered with verbal bandages rather than uncovered for inspection.

It seems clear – not every general statement needs a survey to buttress it – that those who have been trained in the ancient and modern literatures, in philosophy, in history, may be a little less likely than others to give themselves to the worst excesses of the vicious rhetorics, though in my experience natural scientists are often, linguistically, more austere than their colleagues in the faculty of humanities. It is likely that those who spend much time reading current literature in the social sciences will be deeply influenced by the vicious modes, though there are some excellent writers in this field; and the nineteenth-century fathers of the

social sciences did not fall below the general standards of educated prose.*
'Education,' a strange combination of psychology, sociology, the history
of ideas, and other disciplines, offers without question the finest examples of parasense, though there are some distinguished exceptions. Much
more serious, some of our undergraduate students, and these often the
most intelligent, arrive already practised in vicious rhetoric. How refresh-
ing it is to come across an undergraduate who is merely semi-literate!
He cannot spell, he links singular verbs to plural subjects, his participles
dangle freely, he punctuates according to no discernible system, his
switches of tense and mood are startling ... . Such faults can be corrected
and better habits can be taught. But the undergraduate whose rhetoric
is vicious, who commands a free-flowing style without grammatical er-
rors or mistakes in spelling, whose performance may well have been
praised when he was a schoolboy – what are we to do with him? It is
hard to convict him of sin, for he is filled with a sense of his own right-
eousness; and he can justly claim that the way he writes is modelled on
the practice of those who are older and better-educated than he, perhaps
even on the practice of those who write his textbooks.

It is interesting to note that in the turbulent period of the late 'sixties
there was a vivid contrast between what was published – on walls, in
pamphlets and flyers, in newspapers – by the students revolting in
France and those in Britain and North America. The writings of the
French students were well-organized, witty, and (granted the premisses
of the arguments) compelling: splendid testimonials to the excellence of
the educational system they were denouncing.[2] The writings of the
English-speaking students were, with some (though not many) exceptions, diffuse, vague, full of the clichés of bad writing in sociology,
whining, soaked in self-pity; they attempted the grand style but the effects were comic.[3] I do not think the reasons for these different performances are hard to find. In the traditional French educational system
there are long years devoted to the reading and analysis of a great body
of French literature that abounds in models, stylistically different, of

---

* It should be said that in the University of Toronto political economy and political
science are professed by distinguished writers.

good writing. *Explication de texte* is an art insisted upon and continually practised. A clever French student in his final year at a good *lycée* can write a piece which, though it may not positively shout for publication, is nevertheless printable. In Britain and North America most undergraduates are in this respect relatively untrained; they will have had a more relaxed life than the French, more fun; even in England where examinations count for much more than they do in North America, there is nothing to compare with the ordeal of the *bachot*. But the consequence for the English-speaking undergraduate is that, lacking any critical sense of the language, he may on the foundation of bad habits already acquired erect some extravagant structure after the fashion of such masters of obscure prose as Marcuse and the translators of the works of the Frankfurt School (notably those of Ernst Bloch) and the general run of writing in sociology.

Here, then, there seems to be a direct connexion between modes of early education and the range and degree of command of language. There is very much more to be said. Perhaps not many of those now entering the universities come from homes where there are many books, where reading and writing are ordinary and common occupations, and where the amount of television viewing is restricted. Such children enter schools, and later universities, at a great disadvantage, as compared with those from bookish homes. (It has to be said that the difference between the bookish and non-bookish home, never altogether a matter of social and economic class, is not now the same difference as that between the middle-class and the working-class home.) All the same, this cannot be the whole story. Anyone who has examined the writing of young children (of course, especially where the teachers are sympathetic) up to the age of nine or ten will have noticed how fresh, original, direct, moving, such writing often is. Just as there is an age of artistic puberty, when children whose drawing and painting have been dazzling in their courage and power fall into a kind of hack routine and imitate the most lifeless academic painting, so there seems to be a disastrous age of literary puberty. My guess is that children gradually come to know what the adult preferences are and fall in with them, in writing, as in painting and drawing. Much of this represents the power of the wider society, with its charac-

teristic vulgarizing of words and images in advertising and cheap periodical literature. Many teachers in our schools know all this; many of them
are discouraged, perhaps as much by the indifference of colleagues as by
the surface resistance of the children. The hard, bitter fact is that universities turn out graduates with decent grades and a fair training in
languages, their own and others, who have no strong interest in the life
of the mind and are unable to give to children what they do not have
themselves. I will not say they never open a serious book once they have
left the university, though of some of them I believe this to be true; but
they have not been infected with any intellectual or artistic passion at
the university; they are consumed by the ambitions of the suburban
middle class. For this the universities must take some share of the responsibility. There must be something about our teaching arrangements,
about the actual teaching, about the methods of assessment, that should
be scrutinized.

It would be a mistake to think poorly of the hopes and ambitions of
undergraduates when they first enter the university. Many of them, no
doubt, have been on the escalator of education since kindergarten and
are astonished to find themselves at the university (or perhaps do not notice that their lives are changed). Some ought to get off the escalator at
this point and go in for another way of life (a liberal education is not
salvation); and some do. But for many the awakening really is an intellectual awakening, and these, like those others who *wanted* to come to
the university, may conceive a romantic love for the place, a love that
will appropriately (like its analogue) be disappointed. An undergraduate
may expect to find an institution of the kind set out for us by Newman.

> ... a University consists, and has ever consisted, in demand and
> supply, in wants which it alone can satisfy, and which it does satis-
> fy, in the communication of knowledge, and the relation and
> bond which exists between the teacher and the taught. Its consti-
> tuting, animating principle is this moral attraction of one class of
> persons to another; which is prior in its nature, nay commonly in
> its history, to any other tie whatever; so that, where this is want-
> ing, a University is alive only in name, and has lost its true essence,

whatever be the advantages, whether of position or of affluence, with which the civil power or private benefactors contrive to encircle it. ... Consideration, dignity, wealth, and power, are all very proper things in the territory of literature; but they ought to know their place; they come second, not first; they must not presume, or make too much of themselves; or they had better be away. First intellect, then secular advantages, as its instruments and as its rewards; I say no more than this, but I say no less.[4]

Again, Newman maintained

that the personal influence of the teacher is able in some sort to dispense with an academical system, but that system cannot in any sort dispense with personal influence. With influence there is life, without it there is none; if influence is deprived of its due position, it will not by those means be got rid of, it will only break out irregularly, dangerously. An academical system without the personal influence of teachers upon pupils, is an arctic winter; it will create an ice-bound, petrified, cast-iron University and nothing else.[5]

A little later he continues, and here he is crying out as though the wounds left by some of his Oxford experiences were still open:

I have known a time in a great School of Letters, when things went on for the most part by mere routine, and form took the place of earnestness. I have experienced a state of things, in which teachers were cut off from the taught as by an insurmountable barrier; when neither party entered into the thoughts of the other; when each lived by and in itself; when the tutor was supposed to fulfil his duty, if he trotted on like a squirrel in his cage, if at a certain hour he was in a certain room, or in hall, or in chapel, as it might be; and the pupil did his duty too, if he was careful to meet his tutor in the same room, or hall, or chapel, at the same certain hour; and when neither the one nor the other dreamed of seeing each other out of lecture, out of chapel, out of academical gown. I have known places where a stiff manner, a pompous voice, coldness and condescension, were the teacher's attributes. ... This was the reign of Law without Influence, System without Personality.[6]

I believe more undergraduates (and, indeed, graduate students as well) than one might imagine have in their minds some such conception of the university as underlies Newman's critical remarks. They know there is a huge distinction between teaching and instruction; they are dissatisfied with the great 'cop-out' they may have come across in their schooldays: that on the foundation of little reading, little information, little practice in argument (I mean, as distinct from assertion and counter-assertion), they have a duty to form opinions on a great variety of subjects, a duty to, as they say, 'make up their own minds for themselves.' They hope to find in the university and through the great men they believe to be its gods moments of epiphany, deeper knowledge, more complex emotion, the unriddling of riddles, maps to many countries of the mind, spells to drive away dragons. I believe that even under the worst conditions, even in the most frozen, petrified, cast-iron institutions, some young men and women do find all these things, despite the circumstances that conspire against them. But many miss them who might have found them, had our internal arrangements been different. I am therefore committed to saying something about some of the things that are wrong and reformable in our teaching and examining arrangements and in the general way in which we conduct our lives as teachers and students in colleges and universities.

In many North American universities and colleges the undergraduate, to earn his bachelor's degree, has to gain twenty or so credits in respect of twenty or so courses or their equivalent in half-courses, and this over a period of four years. These courses may be in varying degrees miscellaneous, though an attempt is sometimes made, often under great difficulties, to give the courses some kind of shape and to encourage a degree of specialization. This can be done by a complicated system of prerequisites for taking particular courses, though there may be disputes over what is to count as a prerequisite, and exceptions are sometimes made at the discretion of the teacher, often called the 'instructor.' (It is curious that the term *instructor* is so generally used, sometimes where it makes sense – students are indeed instructed in Anglo-Saxon and formal logic – sometimes in cases where, though there may be an element of instruction in the teaching, it makes much less sense, as in courses connected with the critical study of literature or philosophy.) But programmes are often disturbingly miscellaneous. I recall seeing in student transcripts from perfectly respectable institutions in the United States such curious combinations as: Greek philosophy, Physical Education, Appreciation of Art, American history, Psychology, Political Science I, Religious Studies, and the like. This is to consider a university

a sort of bazaar or pantechnicon, in which wares of all kinds are heaped together for sale in stalls independent of each other; and that, to save the purchasers the trouble of running about from shop to shop ... whereas ... a University is the home, it is the mansion-house, of the goodly family of the Sciences, sisters all, and sisterly in their mutual dispositions.[7]

If it were possible to get a good liberal education in this way there could be no objection to such a method of ordering university studies. But is it possible?

It strikes me as being in general impossible, though one would not wish to be positive about what is possible for individuals. People of energy, resource, and talent can educate themselves under the most unfavourable conditions. But we have to be concerned with common instances, with those whose ambitions may be encouraged or blighted by a particular university regimen.

The following seem to be objections. Five courses a year leave little margin for leisure, especially in North America where it is customary for undergraduates to spend a large part of the vacation period in non-academic work. Reading outside the lists of prescribed books, profitable musing and dreaming, attendance at meetings of societies and at lectures not prescribed in the curriculum, these things are hard to do. Intellectual curiosity becomes a liability, unplanned, undirected browsing in a library a risky activity.

It is often a part of the growth of the mind to conceive a passion for one particular line of thought. Sometimes such a passion has to be checked; sometimes an undergraduate has to be reminded that something is better kept back for graduate study. But such an interest in one particular line of inquiry may be a sign of swelling maturity and ought to be encouraged. Under the present system one would hesitate to be encouraging, for it would be unwise for a student to earn himself an A + in one course if in his other courses he earns C s or D s.

There is an excessive and undignified concern with grades and averages. Some of this concern, though not all of it, comes from the use made of grading results by the professional schools. If an undergraduate wants to enter (for example) a law school, it is natural he should be concerned with his grade average. He knows, too, or perhaps he suspects, that a small difference in grade average that has no necessary connexion with the relative merits of candidates, but has everything to do with chance, may determine whether or not he enters the law school.

It is risky to generalize about teaching and examining in undergraduate courses in the faculty of humanities or of social science. Teachers and subjects are necessarily different; some teachers are masters of the Socratic method, others are not good at this but are masters of clear exposition; the requirements of a course on the French drama of the seventeenth century or the English novel of the nineteenth are different from those of a course concerned with Plato's theory of knowledge or Hume's natural theology. Above all, styles of teaching are determined in great measure by the size of the class. A class of 150 makes the transition from lecture to dialogue impossible, with a class of forty it is difficult but possible, with a class of ten it would be absurd not to pass swiftly from lecture to dialogue. All the same, I have the impression that, notwithstanding these many variations, many undergraduates see as a required or safe method in the handling of essays and examination answers the regurgitation of material given to them by their teachers. (I may add that here I speak from the bitterness of my English experience as well as my experience in North America.) I am convinced that the only way to break this wretched attitude, with the rewards it seems to offer for toadyism and retentiveness, is to break the present relations between teaching, the content of the syllabus, and the writing of essays and examination answers.

This is not a complete list of what seems to me objectionable in common university practice in the teaching of undergraduates. There is here an entire world of interrelated difficulties, and I suspect that only surgery can cure the disease, though, as is always the case when the knife cuts deep into the vital organs, there is no guarantee that the patient will not die of the operation.

About graduate study in the humanities faculty I have much less to say. Given the equipment of graduates when they come out of the undergraduate school, I think the present programmes are just about what is required; certainly, the organization of the graduate school in North America is more imaginative and more sympathetic in its ethos than anything to be found in Great Britain. Most classes are small enough for the teaching to be properly informal, regurgitation is less possible and is not encouraged; there is a good chance that sound habits of work will be established, powers of speculation encouraged, language and style purified. Anxieties must centre on the selection of topics for theses and on the writing of theses.

It is usual in most universities to include in the statutory requirements for satisfactory work in the writing of a doctoral thesis mention of two things: the work must show evidence of originality and/or it must add to knowledge; and it must contain matter worthy of publication. I think these requirements are burdensome and inappropriate to young men and women at this stage of their careers and I think they are often taken in a Pickwickian sense (more unreality). It is true that we do sometimes come across a thesis which is dazzling in its grasp of the materials and in its originality. But I don't think the *system* can justify itself by such exceptional achievements. The candidates are not yet mature enough, for the most part, and the need to search out some topic that has not yet been covered by monographs or in the professional periodicals may inhibit the full exercise of their powers. It may be convenient here, though my proposals for the reform of undergraduate education come in the next chapter, to set out briefly what I think can be done to mend matters.

If we look at the French system as it was until at least the day before yesterday we find a useful model. The Diploma which entitles the student to teach as a professor at a *lycée* is awarded in respect of a dissertation, a bit shorter than most of our doctoral theses, on which the student works for a year in almost complete freedom. He has a supervisor, but his acquaintance with him may be rather formal and the meetings few. It is not necessary to choose some rather remote subject not covered by monographs or by the periodical literature. Simone Weil, for example, wrote on 'Science and Perception in Descartes,' a subject on which much has been written.[8] (It is true, she only got a low passing mark from the great Brunschvicg; history may remember him for this.) The intention of such a system is to make sure that the student can work systematically in some central, important area of a discipline. It is the crown of a general education in a particular subject or branch of a subject. (It stands far away indeed from such examples, not always legendary, as 'The Use of the Comma in *Tristram Shandy*.)' The assumption of the French practice is that in the case of a young man or woman going into secondary education or into university teaching what is important is not demonstrated research ability in a specialized field but a thorough grasp of, an easy familiarity with, the subject(s) the student will be concerned with as a teacher. It would be absurd (so, I think, this practice implies) to have secondary-school university teachers whose specialized knowledge was prodigious but whose general culture was deficient.

This is not an adequate discussion of North American practice in graduate work. Much could be said in defence of it. It might be argued that trivial and empty subjects do not get past the scrutinizing committees in history or the languages or classics or philosophy or medieval studies. It might be said that I am applying to the whole of graduate work criticisms that get their sharpness from the practice of some schools of education and social science; and that this is unfair. Even if there is something in this, the propriety, or rather the wisdom, of the system remains questionable. The requirement that the thesis should add to the existing store of knowledge (as distinct from offering an interesting interpretation of what is already known) still seems to me dubious, and is in any case perpetually being read in a Pickwickian sense. There is a confusion in the graduate schools between the notion of the doctorate as 'a certificate of competence in the professional role of college teacher' and as 'a recognition of the successful completion of an original contribution to scholarship and knowledge.'[9] I agree with Robert Paul Wolff's suggestion that the doctoral programme in its present form should be abolished and that in its place we should put something more like the French *agrégation*. I make this proposal only to the faculty of humanities, though I suspect it applies with equal force to the faculty of social science. In place of the Doctor of Philosophy degree we should put

a three-year professional degree designed to certify candidates as competent to teach their subjects at the college or graduate level. The requirements for the degree should include intensive course work, independent study, some practice teaching under supervision, and perhaps one or more lengthy pieces of written work. But *no* dissertation![10]

The Doctor of Philosophy degree could then be a distinction awarded, perhaps rarely, as the D. Litt. is, and to those who, already in the middle of their careers as teachers, are moved to creative or scholarly work that deserves this kind of distinction.

A reason for departing here from my intention to attempt in this chapter only criticism and diagnosis, leaving proposals for reform to the next, is that our reflection on graduate work discloses a fundamental problem for those who teach in or have directing positions in modern universities. What they attempt is at once over ambitious and too grovelling; we think that by machinery we can ensure the highest excellence; and imprisoned within the machinery we have established we are preoccupied with the keeping up of minimum standards. Once again, I have to say that there are in the universities extraordinary men and women who are able to transcend the most difficult circumstances of learning; for these there is no law. But to most of those who enter the universities with high hopes, great talent, and good will, we have a duty to arrange our requirements as sensibly as possible. The peril in which we stand is, to use Newman's expression already cited, 'the reign of Law without Influence, System without Personality.'

Any large and complicated society is one society in virtue of its having rules by which we distinguish what is authoritative from what is not. Even a society aspiring to the happy condition in which laws rather than men rule needs men to interpret the laws and to decide on their application to particular situations. A university is such a society; and even if one takes the point of Paul Goodman's remark that 'it is impossible to consider our universities in America without being powerfully persuaded of the principle of anarchy,'[11] one has to conclude that the co-existence of limited supplies of teachers and time, of rooms and paper, and of everything else the university needs, imposes upon us the need to set priorities and settle disputes. Further, in so far as there is and, for many reasons, has to be a close relation of dependence between the university and the political community, there have to be ways of communicating the views of the two sides, that is, there have to be committees and individual office holders who can give an account of the university's housekeeping, and justify it. All universities use the presidential system in one form or another, from the long-term presidents and vice-chancellors of the North American and modern British universities to the temporary and limited presidencies of Oxford and Cambridge. It is certain, therefore, that in universities as in states and business corporations there will be two problems: that of authority (who decides what); and the tendency of the administration to go beyond the limits set by the actual needs of the institution in question (the problem of bureaucracy).

We are less thoughtful about the problem of authority than we were at the end of the 1960s, when universities erupted, buildings were occupied, records ransacked, confidential correspondence stolen and published, and there were confrontations, at times bloody, between demonstrating students and the police and other representatives of the traditional authorities. What is curious is that this was a general phenomenon throughout the western world and on both sides of the Iron Curtain. This means that many of the individual causes advanced as explanations of student revolt may have been necessary, but none was sufficient. I do not propose to guess about the multiple causes of this general crisis. A general explanation would involve calling up such a doubtful hypothesis as that of the *Zeitgeist;* certainly, there *was* a spirit of the time, though it seems to have vanished as swiftly as it came; we have passed from the stormy 'sixties to the stolid 'seventies. What seems fairly evident and hard to quarrel with is that the crisis of authority within the universities was a particular instance of a more general crisis: within families, within churches, within the political community; and we seem driven to suppose that, when all the particular causes for the particular crises have been counted, there remains a vast residue of the unknown; and it seems plausible to believe that the dark history of western society, from the War of 1914-18, through economic depression and the rise of the totalitarian societies, through the age of the massacres, the second World War, the first use of nuclear weapons, the swelling irrationalism represented at its most extreme by the widespread belief in absurd racial doctrines and at its most degradingly trivial by the rise of such superstitions as astrology, that all these things have been so corrosive in their effects that the deference owed to age and experience and to existing authorities in church and state no longer seems natural or justifiable. This seems right, but unspecific. Human institutions can take only so much punishment.

What perhaps ought to surprise us is that out of this chaos so much that has form and beauty has survived. Form and beauty have their own intrinsic authority. To hear Schnabel playing the Beethoven piano sonatas, even through the old recordings, is to perceive authority. To look at some shapes, either at the natural shapes of seashells and flowers and insects, the peacock and the elephant, or at the great cathedrals and humanized landscapes of Europe, or at the vernacular tradition of civility that shows itself in the white frame houses, the tiny neo-classical court houses, of many a small town in North America, this is to recognize authority. Authority in society has always had difficulty in showing itself in such overwhelming, unmistakable ways; and has always therefore striven to make itself perceptible in the way natural shapes and the products of art are perceptible. The crown and the sceptre, the mitre and crozier, the academic cap and gown, the 'logo' designed for the University of Toronto's sesquicentennial celebrations, are so many attempts to render authority perceptible. For those who no longer share in a common symbolic system the enterprise of manifesting authority, verbally or in what is perceptible, is difficult, and this absence of a common stock of symbols is certainly one ground of the crisis of authority. But we still share, despite the influence of vicious rhetorical modes, a common language; if we have the word, the two-fold logos, and keep it fresh through our study of that literature which is man's history, 'his Life and Remains,' then we have in principle a way of coming through our difficulties. By talking? Yes, by talking. To those who object, I would reply in the words, though (I hope) not in the spirit, of the man derided for selling pills to cure the Lisbon earthquake: What else would you suggest?

As to the inherent tendency of administration to go beyond the needs of the society whose service alone justifies its existence, and to find its fulfilment in its own independent growth and aggrandizement, I need only say that there is plainly such a tendency. My guess is that it is hard to halt this growth by a direct attack; the sad consequence may be that we try to cure the evil by adding another tier, or arm, to the existing structure. (The history of bureaucracy in the Communist states is worth study in this respect. The 'struggle against bureaucracy' is one of the earliest political catchwords; and the cure is the establishment of a variety of commissions and other bodies whose responsibility it is to administer the bureaucratic spirit out of existence; what in fact happens is that routine measures to eliminate bureaucracy become themselves a part of the ever-expanding bureaucratic system.) Perhaps if we were to decide what kind of an institution a university is and how its intellectual life is best ordered, and we were to make the right decisions, we should cure the worst evils of bureaucracy incidentally. I maintain that a university is a 'natural' institution (rather in the sense in which Aristotle thought the *polis* natural) and that if we can arrive at some agreement over what should be done within it and how best this may be done, we shall find the problems of excessive and burdensome administration solving themselves.

In all human societies the young want to know how to do certain things and what the truth is about man and God and society and Nature. The *studia generalia* have been systematic attempts to provide the space within which the young can ask those who are older how to set about satisfying these two kinds of inquiry. The city as well as the university is the setting within which such questions are raised. As Newman notes, the city is a university of a kind. But the university proper is the best way so far hit upon 'for the education of youth into universal culture.'[12] It also initiates them into the practice of this culture; this, at least, is the point, the idea of the university. The world is hungry for such practitioners and it seems a pity to disappoint this world. It is stuffing itself at the moment with what is provided by the fashionable gurus of the hour. But what they give us does not sustain life and may even be poisonous.

IV

Some
Proposals
for Change
and Reform

In treating reform and change I propose to limit the field of discussion. I shall give most attention to undergraduate education, and ever since Flexner[1] this has ceased to be thought, in most of North America, a primary responsibility of the university. So far Canada has been different, though even here disgraceful proposals for doing undergraduate education on the cheap and devoting what has been stolen from undergraduate education to 'research' surface from time to time. Indeed, undergraduate education can be done, and is often done very well, in the liberal arts college, outside the university proper. I think this is the great weakness of the North American university and was a cause – though not *the* cause – of some of the feeling of estrangement that began to come over the undergraduate body in the 'sixties. It strikes me as quite intolerable that, as happens in some American universities, first-year teaching should be done by the most junior instructors and by graduate students. (The imaginative use of graduate students in teaching is one of the most attractive features of American universities.)* It is from the undergraduate body that the leavening element in society, or one of those elements at least, will come, as well as the future university and high school teachers. They deserve to be treated as seriously as graduate students and the work of research. If they are thought to be a distraction from the serious and main business of the professor they will know this – their antennae are sensitive. But in the English and Canadian traditions the argument need not be insisted on. That the university has pastoral responsibilities has not hitherto been seriously questioned. I suspect that undergraduates who declaim against paternalism would not really relish being put into the situation of an undergraduate student in Paris or Berlin. That they would never be placed in double jeopardy (that is, subject both to the disciplinary jurisdiction of the university and to the ordinary courts of law) would in time come to seem far from agreeable. In any case, neither parents nor government would here tolerate such a thing for a moment, nor, I believe, would the mass of undergraduates. To take the lowest ground, it would involve the dismantling of all the special social services provided by the university; if the university is to be simply a provider of specific services, like a bank or a municipality, then there is no reason for the provision of amenities additional to those provided for the rest of the community.

Again, I make no proposals for the reform of committee structures or for detailed changes in administration. Some of my proposals would, were they to be accepted, involve changes in these matters; and there can be little doubt that a principal difficulty any proposals for reform are likely to meet is the need for changes that may disturb established and cherished modes of administration.

The university is a 'natural' institution; here is the starting-point. Nature; convention: these are difficult concepts and the history of philosophy is in part an account of their complexities and ambiguities. Eating is a natural practice and the formal occasions and styles of eating are by

* One might add that the general use made of graduate and undergraduate students in a great variety of domestic and administrative tasks is something from which Europe could learn much.

derivation natural institutions; they satisfy human needs at both the biological level (we eat to live) and at the social level (eating together as members of families, as friends and lovers, as members of a multitude of fraternities and sororities, satisfies more complex appetites; but these appetites may be called needs if we allow that civility is a virtue and civilization a set of devices for living well). That something is done by convention, that we eat turkey at Thanksgiving or goose at Christmas, does not mean that what is done is unnatural. To satisfy a human as distinct from a purely animal need is to do something the style and content of which is invented and therefore exists by convention as well as by nature, for how the human need is met is different in China from how it is in Peru. Some ways of eating – all those that are simply, as it were, calls at some filling station – fall below the human level; others may stretch towards gluttony and be below the human level in a different way: the ancient Roman institution of provoking vomiting in order to begin again is both unnatural and, as we say, beastly, though of all the animals only man can be beastly with such ingenuity.

Teaching and learning constitute a natural relation, one that is needed for survival – much that is in the other animals instinctive (such as swimming) is with us learned behaviour – and, once survival is safeguarded, for satisfying the needs of civilization. That moral attraction between the generations to which Newman refers, that bond between the teacher and the taught, is, where it finds expression, a sign of health. One understands why among the Greeks the relation is portrayed through the image of an erotic relationship and is also thought, by a metaphor, to be a kind of midwifery.

The former – the erotic – is brought out by a charming passage in a pseudo-Platonic dialogue in which a young man speaks to Socrates in the following terms:

> I made progress when I associated with you, even if I was only in the same house, though not in the same room; but more so when I was in the same room with you; and I seemed to myself to improve much more, when, being in the same room, I looked at you,

when you were speaking, than when I looked another way. But I made by far the greatest progress, when I sat near you and touched you.[2]

Here we have a culture, an ethos, very different from the culture and ethos of the somewhat repressed and inhibited Anglo-Saxon societies. It is closer to the world of the New Testament, where the relation of master to disciple may be represented as tactual, the touching of a garment's hem, the washing of feet. And the role of the teacher on the Socratic model is to be a midwife, to assist the soul to bring into the world that which it is already big with. Teaching here is not instruction; at least, though the element of instruction may always be there, it is not the principal element in the teaching relation.

If we try to bring these principles to bear on particular cases, then the difference between teaching and instruction would be something like this. It may be rightly thought that all those who have grown up within a particular community, with its cultural traditions and above all with its own natural language which is itself a register of the past, have within themselves a store of what is potentially knowledge: knowledge of matters of fact, knowledge of how to handle problems, knowledge of the depth and complexity of human character, knowledge of good and evil, knowledge of those necessary structures of the world and of discourse that are when fully developed logic and mathematics and perhaps physics. We find ourselves and our world in literature and history and philosophy and natural science; and we do not have to resort to any theory of the recollection of a previous existence to account for our knowledge. We encounter *Othello* and *Macbeth* as revelations because we have already known the pains of jealousy and the misery of ambition fulfilled and then thwarted. Freud's greatness lies in his having perceived this and in his having seen that the art of healing is precisely the art of teaching, that is, it is maieutic, it brings out of the patient or pupil that which is already there, dark, chaotic on first appearance, unformulated (or improperly, deceptively formulated). The form of communication from which we may hope for enlightenment is *indirect*. Maieutic teaching consists above all in the telling of stories in which the learner finds himself and his problems. Whatever the teacher does must be directed towards allowing the story to do its own work; always – Look at this, and this, and ... What do you think? How does it strike you? Does it remind you of something? Ideally one would never resort to direct communication: *this* is what the story means, *this* is the appropriate feeling, *this* is what on my authority as a teacher you ought to think. Such a method has a wider application than we are at first inclined to suppose. It applies to the teaching of certain branches of the law. The experimental method in the natural sciences is essentially such a method, for it removes attention from the person of the teacher to the structure of the world taken as a story with a meaning.[3] Speculative questions can scarcely be elucidated in any other way. For instance, we are sometimes prompted to ask: Are the rules of arithmetic as they are because of how the world happens to be? (This is not a strange question if we reflect that the discovery of the non-Euclidean geometries long preceded the discovery that they had cosmic application. (The way to compel an answer to the question about the rules of arithmetic is to reply (here the debt to Wittgenstein is obvious): Try to imagine how the world would have to be for the rules of arithmetic to change. Could this be imagined? Here is a request for a story. If the pupil remains unresponsive, the correct way to approach him would be to tell a story, e.g. If every time you put x marbles into a container five minutes later – five? O Lord! think about that! – you always extracted $x - 1$. ... Or again: Imagine the circumstances in which an intuitively obvious principle such as that there can be no greatest whole number would be falsified. ... I need not multiply examples.

Now, I do not argue that this is the sole allowable method in university teaching. Of course, there has to be instruction, though the more pupils can be given books and told to instruct themselves the better. What I maintain is that this is in liberal education the *central* method and the only one that has transforming power. So long as this is kept in mind, we shall pick up a species of spiritual tact, inserting the instruction where and only where it is needed. It is, of course, a method that carries with it enormous dangers, for such teaching may be profoundly disturbing. The method of the Sophists, the art of making friends and influencing people, the acquisition of slogans and mnemonics, always seems in the short run to be safer and more profitable; but it leaves the pupil dried up, ripe only as a prune is ripe, stuffed with trivialities, a comfortable member of the mass, neither saint nor sinner, neither hot nor cold, neither Socrates nor Alcibiades.

Our task, if my account of the teaching relationship is roughly right, is to make teaching possible and to keep instruction in its modest, proper place. In this belief the following suggestions are made. Let the present system of a multiplicity of courses and half-courses in respect of which grades are given and recorded be abolished, except, perhaps, for the first year of undergraduate study. In the first year not more than four courses should be required, and in the case of those already committed to a specialized 'honours' programme not more than three. By the end of the first year students should be required to choose either to enter a specialized programme or to register for a further two years for a three-year 'pass' degree. (There would have to be arrangements for transfer to meet the needs of those who came to repent of this choice.) An honours or specialized programme is either a single-subject programme or a programme with a 'major' subject and a 'minor.' Some subjects such as English or French or German language and literature strike me as naturally providing single-subject programmes. English or French or German necessitates the study, not only of literature and language narrowly considered, but also of history, philosophy, religion. Imagine a study of Racine which did not bring in Pascal and Port-Royal, or a study of Milton that was not also concerned with the theology and politics of seventeenth-century Puritanism. Philosophy, in my view, ought always to be either a major or a minor, never a single-subject programme, simply because it is highly desirable to have some material to philosophize about. Study within an honours programme would be progressive and cumulative and its content would be fixed by a published syllabus and booklist. These would function as guides throughout the years of study. (In practice, there would have to be provisions for options, transfers, emerging anomalies, and what have you. These I need not discuss.)

Teaching would take two forms. In the first place, there would be classes to which the student would be committed in virtue of his having chosen the programme. They would never be lecture courses, or only rarely and exceptionally, but would take the form of seminars or tutorials. All students would be required to do a great deal of essay writing throughout the course – not less than one essay each week. No grades would be awarded during the three years, though students would be told formally at the end of the second and third years how they were doing: that their work showed promise of distinction; that it was satisfactory; that it was weak or unsatisfactory (this would entail the giving of a warning).

In the second place, there would be a programme of lectures by members of the faculty. Suggestions and proposals for lecture courses would be invited. No lecture course would attempt to 'cover the ground' with a view to helping students to prepare for the final examination. Faculty members would be encouraged to lecture on topics in which they were especially interested or on which they were doing work. For instance (to think ahead with some freedom), there might be sets of ten or more lectures on such subjects as 'The English Reformation 1509-1549,' 'The Origins of the Arthurian Legends,' 'The Epic: with special reference to the Icelandic Sagas,' 'The Natural Theologies of Berkeley and Hume compared and contrasted,' 'The Comic: with special reference to Dickens, W.W. Jacobs, Leacock, and Wodehouse,' 'Don Quixote and the Giants *or* The Decline of Chivalry,' 'Concept and Object: a reappraisal of Frege,' 'Parkman on the Old Regime in Quebec: a reassessment,' 'Problems in American Indian Theology,' 'Flaubert and Zola: the Aesthetics of Naturalism,' 'The two Fausts, Goethe's and Marlowe's,' 'The Theory and Practice of ancient Greek Medicine' ... . There would have to be a committee to review the year's offerings in advance, to look after such questions as those of duplication and lack of balance within the programme and to inquire about the more curious and puzzling proposals and discuss them with their authors. Attendance at these lectures would not be required; and it seems probable that, deprived of a captive audience, some sets of lectures would die early in the term. I see no objection to this. Adam Smith has some wise words to say on the topic.

No discipline is ever requisite to force attendance upon lectures which are really worth the attending, as is well known wherever any such lectures are given. ... Such is the generosity of the greater part of young men, that so far from being disposed to neglect or despise the instructions of their master ... they are generally inclined to pardon a great deal of incorrectness in the performance of his duty, and sometimes even to conceal from the public a good deal of gross negligence.[4]

While attendance at lectures would not be required, students would be encouraged to range outside their major field as well as advised to attend particular lectures within the field. This is, I conceive, a liberating proposal for members of the faculty. They would be freed to *teach;* and they would be able to lecture on what interested them. It would be normal, though not obligatory, to offer a set of lectures in, say, every other year, though it would be possible to arrange that those who lectured in a given year would do proportionately less tutoring and that those who did not would do more.

If grades are to be got rid of and the whole conception of constructing a degree course out of twenty or so building blocks is to be rejected, how are the performances of students to be assessed? By means of a final examination. The justification of the final examination is that a university course is cumulative; the whole thing is of a piece; what follows the second year or the third year builds upon what has already been accomplished. I am satisfied that where the building-block system prevails what is learned in XYZ 295 is commonly, though not invariably, forgotten when other courses are begun. What is accumulated under pressure and committed to memory is *discharged* in examinations and term papers; and there is rarely a sufficient motive later on to recover what was discharged; the grade remains, the performance is over, what was acquired becomes a dim memory having no relation to the process of learning extended over the three or four years. (Perhaps it ought to be emphasized again that here there is no intention to deny the existence of the energetic, gifted and fortunate student whose achievement contradicts all generalizations.)

The form of the final examination is a matter for much reflection. The English model of eight or nine three-hour papers in which the candidates write three or four essay-type answers on each paper is in itself criticizable and in any case probably does not travel well to North America. What I myself would favour would be, say, three papers of this kind, a couple of long essays, and rigorous and formally constructed *viva-voce* examinations. The final assessment of a candidate's merit would take into account tutors' reports, though I think it would be sound to lay it down that such reports should in no cases be allowed to depress an otherwise good performance. As to the classifying of examination results, I think there is a lot to be said for a two- or three-class system, without refined sub-divisions: a small first class and a large second class within which there will congregate candidates very different in achievement, and a safety-net for those whose performance is poor, though they have not been notably delinquent. Whether such candidates should be given a third-class or a pass degree seems not a matter to stick over.

There are many corollaries of such a system as I propose and many consequences, some of them foreseeable, some not. Among the corollaries I single out the need for the individual student to be given an academic home. If education is, as I have argued, spread through a network of 'natural' relations between teacher and taught, older and younger, then it needs institutional expression and support. Here I see the function of the colleges and the departments. Each college should have a strong representation of the principal departments (individual colleges might specialize in subjects not so greatly in demand) and the department in the college would be the home, academically speaking, of the undergraduate student. This is where he should be able to meet with and talk to senior members of the department in which he is specializing or majoring and to the undergraduates with whom he is studying. Under our present system many students are, in my view, homeless, unless by chance they hit upon some congenial group or friendly teacher; and such a home is built on frail foundations, for it exists outside the system and to some extent contrary to it. Of course, I know that in Toronto as in many other universities in North America good departments with strong traditions do often function as homes for specializing students; but this too is, as it were, outside the system. Where colleges do not exist, or do not exist as centres of an independent life, the responsibility of departments towards specializing students is even greater. They have in effect to be colleges.

Among the pleasing foreseeable consequences of such a system as that I have outlined – quite apart, that is, from the increase in richness of experience and height of accomplishment that would (if I am right) come about – is the making superfluous of all the anxious administration that is at present required for the collection of grades, their reduction to some common quantitative measure: everything that is involved in what is sometimes called the 'processing' of student records. (If one telephones a provincial or federal government department about a document submitted two months earlier, one is likely to be told that it is still being 'processed.') Such a system would certainly strengthen departments; they would no longer be mere suppliers of the building bricks of a degree programme. They would have greater weight in relation to deans and other academic administrators, if only because they would, with the colleges, be responsible for much of the remaining administrative work that under the present system has to be done outside and between departments and colleges. We should find in such a programme a strengthening of the life of departments and colleges, and these would thus be stronger and more capable of acting as counterweights to the central concerns and administrative power of the university.

There seem to be two major objections to my proposals, one of principle, one merely practical, though if discussion of such proposals were ever to become a serious question within – and, in the end, outside too – the university, the issues of principle and practice would become interwoven. The objection of principle is that what I have proposed is the establishing, within large universities of the kind that, multiversities or not, are committed to the service of the community and serve the community by training people to be everything from historians and philosophers to nurses and accountants, of an elitist liberal arts college. The practical objection is that it would at first and perhaps for long be wildly unpopular among many students; it would be vertigo-inducing, like going up a steep stairway, without banisters or guard-rails, on the outside of a building and in a fierce gale. The opportunity to construct one's degree out of the building blocks, as one goes along, now dropping out wholly or in part, now returning for the full rigour of the five courses a year programme, now catching a convenient course at a summer session, is found useful and valued on that account; this kind of opportunity would be gone. It would also be unpopular among some university teachers and administrators. The sad fact is that the building block system need not be a taxing way of teaching; the system I propose would be taxing and troublesome. The present system makes a good deal of central administration absolutely necessary. Even if my proposals would have a liberating effect on teachers and scholars who unwillingly endure the pains of the present system, there may be others who have grown so accustomed to the system that a break with it would seem the end of a dear and familiar world.

The proposals so far made do not aim at the establishing of an *exclusive* regime for undergraduate studies. There would still have to be a three-year degree, perhaps founded upon some compromise between the old order and the new and deeply affected, one would hope, by the spirit of the new. There are many students, and the community owes them something, who find themselves in 'the higher education sector' without their having ever considered whether or not they want to have a liberal education. To dismiss them altogether from university education seems unkind and is politically impossible; but it would be to their disadvantage and bad for the university to try to bend them to the requirements of the system I have suggested.

That I am proposing to establish within the larger university an elitist liberal arts college I admit. Universities are in any case elitist institutions. If they were not they would have no point and would not be worth the cost to society of maintaining them. By what paths students are to get to the university, and what tests are to be imposed upon them as they advance towards it – ordeals of air, water, fire, fiends such as Apollyon straddling the way – these are important matters of social policy I do not concern myself with here. But once they have arrived at the university, they have the right, I suggest, to choose, after a preliminary year, between the most exacting kind of liberal education, such as I have proposed, and another kind in which instruction would be more prominent, guidance firmer, the structure more flexible, so that students would be able to drop out for a year, drop out partially, make up credits in summer sessions, and so on. I think a great many people would choose the latter; but I am sure enough would choose the former to make it a workable, a sustainable exercise. Much would depend on the inward assent and commitment of the teachers. The teachers would find it exacting, for it would not make possible the clear, precise limit of x hours a week that many value. As it is now, many conscientious teachers go far beyond their prescribed limits; under my proposals they would be working with the system, not trying to counter an illiberal system, and the experience would surely be rewarding.

I have already suggested that under the proposed new scheme of things there would be substantial benefits in the simplifying of administration. Departments would be the collectors and custodians of student records (something most of them already do); and where there are colleges this could be done by the department and the college together. A decentralized administrative system is almost always more frugal, less given to new appointments and the purchase of expensive equipment, than a centralized system, and I should therefore expect my proposals to bring about some saving of money. I do not think it is necessary that teaching costs should rise to balance the economy in administration, though this might happen. It would be a stimulating challenge to the faculty to be told to do what they could without changing existing teacher/pupil ratios, and to be generous in their interpretation of what the new programme would demand.

My great dread, one that I know many share, is that, in the future, proposals for reform, mine or others, would get caught up in a process of collective bargaining between the faculty and the university administration. Conditions of work are obviously pertinent matter in any collective bargaining procedures. This makes evident the pernicious character of such procedures. For the faculty to negotiate with 'the university' is to admit that the faculty is not the university, to abandon the notion of the *universitas*, to accept a proletarian status, not under protest, but as a norm. This is in effect to abandon the entire university tradition and to accept the term *university* as denoting an employing authority, like Bell Canada or Imperial Oil. I suspect many faculty members have fallen into this position inadvertently. Many motives have induced a majority of them – *not* all – to accept collective bargaining as inevitable, perhaps unfortunately so, but nevertheless inevitable given the existing relations between the university and the political authority. Its terrible consequences may be that changes of a purely academic kind, having to do with how we see our educational task, will, simply because they of necessity involve changes in conditions of work, be looked upon in a suspicious spirit, as an attempt of 'them' to put something over on 'us.' To fall into such a frame of mind and to allow it to shape our attitudes and actions is to cheat students, to cheat the community, to cheat ourselves. In effect, it would be analogous to the open abandoning by the medical profession of the provisions of the Hippocratic Oath.

We now have (to resume my dream) a more differentiated university community, in which there are many centres of power and interest; colleges, where these are already established, strong departments no longer wholly concerned with servicing a cafeteria-type system but able to, as it were, produce their own bill of fare. All kinds of tension would exist under this system, sources of irritation, opportunities for idleness and pointless eccentricity, above all there would be *anomalies*. Anomalies seem to make us fidgety and sometimes we have reasonable grounds for our anxieties. But anomalies are simply a part of human life and elaborate machinery to correct them may have worse consequences than putting up with them. For example, in all English universities known to me some honours schools (within and between universities) consistently produce more first-class degrees in proportion to the numbers of candidates than do others. Now, it may be that better candidates present themselves for some subjects rather than others and from some universities rather than others. Who is to say? I do not myself believe this is true. '... At Balliol their geese are always swans,' complained Mark Pattison;[5] but he did not propose a commission of inquiry to look into the practices of the delinquent college. In any case, these things look after themselves. If Firsts in Chinese are always plentiful at the University of Barsetshire, rare at the University of Loamshire, it is the Loamshire graduates, not those of Barsetshire, that will benefit. Referees for academic posts whose reports on candidates are always laudatory and uncritical do not carry much weight. There is here a self-correcting mechanism; no additional mechanism need be imposed. Of course, if, as under our present system, grades have to be homogenized and averaged, then it seems right we should attempt to arrange the grades in a given class along some plausible curve. But this is to produce other anomalies, and those of the worst kind, for they are hidden. The quantification of assigned grades assumes an accuracy and consistency of attitude that, in most subjects in the arts faculty, are not to be had. The homogenizing of grades and their arrangement is more an exercise in public relations than a guarantee that justice has been done. Students know this very well. They know that first-class performances can be picked out, that a broadly satisfactory performance is recognizable, that a bare pass is possible, that failure is commonly unmistakable. But they know that refinements of grading that go beyond such broad divisions are hard or impossible to get right, are subjective in a high degree, and may even be matters of chance.

To return to the question of colleges. My view is that the strength of colleges whose membership may range from, say, 800 to two or three thousand, rests upon two things: the existence of a lively tradition (this is why the first years of a new college are so critical); and the having of a substantial academic role, not as agents of a central authority, but in their own right.

The origin and growth of traditions in small societies is a mysterious business. Any society that has in some degree a life of its own and is distinguishable from the larger societies within which it exists, as the child in the womb relies upon its mother for support and is yet a distinct individual, generates traditions, stories, manners, shared confidences, preferences, into all of which a new member is inducted. This happens without intervention from the outside and without deliberate planning. One sees this in street gangs, religious congregations, families, shops and offices, factories, government departments ... and colleges. Izaak Walton thought that if you left horsehairs in ponds they would breed eels and that the barnacles on ships' bottoms turned into geese of their own accord. Certainly, if you leave a little social group to itself it will quite non-miraculously breed traditions, an atmosphere one can recognize but not always describe with any definiteness. Some degree of independence and some degree of stability of membership and some inducement to remember are all one needs. (This is why senior members of colleges, with a permanent commitment to the institution, are so important.) But for a college more is needed if personality is to be recognized and system kept in its place. The Innis College Principal's Report for 1975-76 is, here in Toronto, a notable reflective account of the making of a matrix of tradition and its adaptation to the transfer of the college to a new home in 1976.

On the Toronto campus the federated colleges derive their traditions from the religious communities by whom they were conceived and from their existence and powers as distinct universities. It would not be the end of them as self-conscious institutions if they were to distance themselves from their religious traditions, as we can see from the many American examples of universities and colleges that were originally sectarian foundations but whose origins are now scarcely remembered. I myself hope this won't happen with my own college, Saint Michael's, in Toronto, though I suspect it may happen with some of the better Catholic colleges and universities in the United States. I was much struck by a passage in Jencks's and Riesman's The Academic Revolution (1968). They wrote, after noting the general tendency of Catholic universities and colleges to emulate the secular universities and colleges, with the possibility that they will in the end be indistinguishable from them:

> The important question ... is not whether a few Catholic universities prove capable of competing with Harvard and Berkeley on the latter's terms, but whether Catholicism can provide an ideology or personnel for developing alternatives to the Harvard-Berkeley model of excellence.[6]

This is not to be evaded or avoided. It offers a stiff challenge to such a college as Saint Michael's. Is there within the tradition of Catholicism a richness capable of offering something that is to others recognizably a contribution to university education and at the same time so distinctive that it is more than simply such a contribution but is as different from what is to be found elsewhere as apples are from oranges? At one time the answer to such a hard question would not have been in doubt. Catholic higher education was often conceived as a means of preserving the faith of young Catholics from a threatening environment. In North America, and especially in the United States, the appetite among Catholics for higher education was great, and there was an especially strong desire to enter such professional schools as those of law and medicine. These were obvious ways of rising up through the hierarchy of American society; and the effect of such desires and pressures has been spectacular, and is especially instanced in the rise of Catholics of Irish origin to the summits of the plutocracy, from humble beginnings two generations ago to the moment when the ascent of John F. Kennedy to the Presidency (or the elevation of Grace Kelly to membership of the princely family of Monaco) seals an era of triumph. It should be noted, though, that JFK was a graduate of Harvard, not of Notre Dame or Boston College. There may be many morals in this.

The presupposition of most of those who founded and encouraged the many Catholic institutions in the United States was that it was possible to provide a Catholic atmosphere within which the humanities – the natural sciences were on the whole not represented with power and distinction – could be studied. It was further believed that there were special Catholic versions of such subjects as history and that the teaching of these versions would equip the young Catholic graduate to engage in effective debate with unbelievers and heretics. Those graduates who had been simple enough to swallow this story swiftly came to see they had been deceived. The general quality of Catholic education was in fact low in the standard subjects, even though here and there, at Notre Dame, at Fordham, at Georgetown, and other places there were commanding and distinguished teachers. Very little theology was studied; this was thought to be primarily a seminary subject – the day of the lay theologian had not yet come – and in any case sensible administrators shrank from the close relations with the Roman congregations that would have been involved in any setting up of formal theological study. Some rather low-grade philosophico-theological instruction did go on in classes given various titles – apologetics, religious knowledge, and so on – and in general this seems to have been poor. It involved, not the study of the Scriptures and the Fathers and such great intellectual ornaments of the Catholic tradition as Aquinas and Scotus and Suarez, but the study of rather sad textbooks, the products of the neo-scholastic movement at its most decadent.

Piety of an individualistic kind was encouraged. Notre Dame was just coming out of the period I have been describing when I paid my first visit there in 1957; but on the eve of a big football game it was still common for the young men to, as it was put, hit the box and hit the rail for Notre Dame.

All this has been chronicled for us by Monsignor John Tracy Ellis, to whose books and articles I refer those interested.[7] It is a distant period, almost infinitely far away from our present situation. Today very few people could be found to maintain there is such a thing as Catholic history except in the sense that there is history written by Catholics; and Catholics may be interested in special periods and topics, just as Protestants or Marxists or secular humanists may be. In ecclesiastical history today there is little substantial difference between Catholics and others. Professor Harry McSorley of Saint Michael's College is an authority on Luther[8] and to my mind his treatment of Luther is more sympathetic than that of some historians who are not Catholics. In the now often ecumenical schools of theology Catholic and Protestant teachers and students jostle each other amiably in the same classes. A somewhat conservative Anglican clergyman who by some strange chance went to study the New Testament at Louvain once complained to me, and this was ten years ago, that it was 'just like Cambridge.' A whole world has died, that of old-style Anglo-Hibernian Catholicism, and not many now mourn its passing.

But how in these changed circumstances is a Catholic college to respond to Jencks's and Riesman's challenge? In effect they are saying to us: Put up or shut up. We can no longer maintain, for our practice contradicts it, that in the general run of subjects in the arts and social sciences we have a distinctive standpoint, a special message to communicate; and plainly it would be absurd to hold – it has always been absurd to hold – that there can be Catholic physics or biology, Catholic engineering or Catholic surgery. Sometimes we clutch at 'atmosphere,' that indefinable but perfectly real factor that goes with the life of institutions, that here in Toronto would make even a secularized Trinity, Victoria, Saint Michael's subtly different to a man with a good nose for atmospheres. (Oxford is not today in any real sense an Anglican or even a Christian university, but to my nose there is all the same an unmistakably Anglican atmosphere about it.) But since we cannot devise atmospheres and since they commonly resist analysis, we must leave them to look after themselves. It seems to me implausible that a decree compelling all priests and religious (for example) to wear soutane or habit when on the Saint Michael's campus, or even within the general area of Queen's Park, would create 'atmosphere,' except in a rather Hollywood sense. (Of course, the *abandoning* of distinctively religious forms of dress has had a profound effect, for good or bad.) Fancy dress, then, is out, a distinctive method and content in the teaching of most subjects is out, only Catholic teachers for exclusively Catholic students has long been out, as Jencks and Riesman discovered, a little to their astonishment, about Saint Michael's back in 1968.[9]

What is left? Is assimilation into the culture of a secularized society inevitable? In another generation will only atmosphere be left? Will the names of Maritain and Gilson, Phelan and Carr, commemorated above doorways on the Saint Michael's campus, be to a future generation of Canadians what the names of Laud and Newman are to modern Oxford?

An honest look at Catholicism today seems to yield, at least to my gaze, two things: a peculiar moral (and implicitly political) outlook; and a special view of the place of *cult* within society. (I leave out of account, as not my business here, the enormous and, to some, offensive claims of the Catholic Church to be the peculiar recipient of and witness to Divine revelation; this is a settled matter for Catholics and I assume it in what I have to say.) There is much in contemporary Catholicism one could, as it were, think away without destroying Catholicism considered as a religious culture. After all, we have lost the liturgical language (I speak only of Catholics of the Latin Rite) of fifteen hundred years; and we survive. But there are two classes of things that, I believe, one cannot think away and, having done so, find that one is still confronted with Catholicism: morality, and cult.* When I do so, I find myself faced with liberal Protestantism or with an agnosticism tinged with Protestant pathos. I feel much closer, almost as though I were a member of the family, to Eastern Orthodoxy or even to Orthodox Judaism than I do to liberal Protestantism. For me, then, the special character of Catholicism shows itself when it sets its face like stone against the killing of the unborn and when it manifests itself, in the person of a John Howard Griffin or a Dorothy Day, in total opposition to the superstitions of racism and the obscene practices of modern warfare, defensive or not. (Aquinas asked long ago *Utrum bellare sit semper peccatum*,[10] and the irony in the question has rarely been perceived.) Again, the special character of Catholicism discloses itself to me in liturgical worship, especially in the worship that surrounds the Eucharistic sacrifice. Here is made present, sacramentally, under and behind the sacramental signs, the celestial life represented for the imagination in the *Paradiso* of Dante. Our conversation is in Heaven. Water, wine, bread, oil, salt, wax, fire, metals, all conspire to bring us body and spirit into the Kingdom. Here I am not saying that the traditional liturgical worship of Latin Catholicism is a great work of art, though it is, and moving in this respect. I want to say, if I may be forgiven the word, something ontological. Here I borrow good words from Peter Levi, from what he said at the Requiem for David Jones (painter, engraver, poet, novelist) in 1975.

> We are doing here what is done elsewhere and what has been done. When the priest comes to the holy words of Christ's institution, to the consecration of the sacrament, his will and his meaning is simply to do what the Church does, there is nothing personal in what he intends, any more than in what he accomplishes. He means what is meant by the assembly of the saints of God in this church. He does in another form what the painters of the caves of Lascaux already did for their fellows, only now substantially. ...

---

* Perhaps I ought to disclose my own deep prejudice and explain that I feel closer to a superstitious old peasant woman lighting candles and kissing icons than to a pious young Protestant brooding on the synoptic problem.

Is it very remote to illuminate the early emergence of man on this planet from what we understand of the Mass? And when the Mass, which really we understand so little, and which alone transforms the universe, has thrown its light into those pure and dark beginnings, how intense or how faint a light does our understanding of man in his beginnings reflect onto this congregation's knowledge of itself? Yet human nature must make some sense; how else can the universe be understood? What is performed here has for its meaning and scope the metamorphosis of mankind. It is the beginning of the marriage supper of the lamb who was sacrificed. ... We are creatures, our service and our remembrance are creaturely. We kiss the cloth on the altar. We shall all die. The Christ who is in this church is the Christ of Stonehenge and of the earliest centuries of mankind, the Christ of every star in the sky, and of every nameless ignorant soldier dying in a wet ditch. He will come to judge the world in fire. He was murdered before the beginning of time. Let us transform ourselves at last, let us enter into that mystery, whatever our measure is our calling is to become Christ.[11]

If I am right in emphasizing the central importance of morality and cult in Catholicism, then there are certain things that seem to follow from this for the regime of a college in this tradition. First, the adherence to a morality different in certain respects from the general ethos of 'western' society has to be shown in some open way. How to do this I leave as an open question. It would seem to me strange if, say, in the conduct of student residences Catholics were to capitulate before the present ethos of spontaneity and self-expression. It is, of course, very hard to be good without being pharisaical; but this is a perennial problem. We have to remember that the tax-gatherers and harlots may go into the Kingdom before the respectable. Secondly, we have to ask ourselves if we give to our liturgical worship all that we, as a society of learned men, with a greater than common knowledge of our tradition as Latin Catholics, made sensitive to the varieties of human experience through the study of letters, practitioners of sacramental religion, can do. Such treasures of the tradition as the chant (men have been converted listening to the Solesmes monks) and the liturgical music of such masters as Byrd and Palestrina – do we value them? Or are we as philistine in this field as we are lovers of sweetness and light in other fields? A Catholic college which reserves its philistinism for all the splendour that traditionally surrounds Catholic worship is surely in a very odd way. There are such offices as Vespers and Compline (combined with some genius by Cranmer into the Anglican office of Evensong), offices that when sung usher us at least into the ante-chambers of heaven. Are they there on the campus for those who want to assist at them? Is our preaching intellectually challenging or does it seem directed towards young men and women who are taken to be ingenious in their approaches to academic subjects but ingenuous in their approaches to the mysteries of faith? I ask these questions; I do not answer them.

I now attempt a summing up of what I have tried to do here. First, I have maintained that the essence of the university is that it is a *studium generale*, an ecumenical institution, and a place of general resort for learned men and for those who seek learning. Then, it is an *universitas*, an independent corporation in charge of its own life. Again, I suggest that in North America generally, and in Canada in particular, the ways in which we arrange our lives of teaching and study are not the best open to us. So far as undergraduate education in the faculty of arts is concerned, I have suggested that we ought to forsake the fragmented system at present favoured, and forsake the building blocks, for the continuous growth of specialized study after the first year. From this there would come a change in the distribution of powers and responsibilities within the university, with colleges and departments absorbing some of the work that is now the business of the central administration. I said much less about graduate study; but I do propose that the doctoral thesis* be abolished and that there be substituted for it a programme that would certify successful candidates as fit to begin teaching in institutions of higher education. About administration I say almost nothing directly. I think if we can get the work of the university right at the level of the

---

* Of course, only as a part of the standard graduate programme.

classroom and the library we shall in fact make the university looser in its structure, having many different centres of power and interest, more sparing in its use of administrative resources. (Of course, as being responsible for the administration of much property and for the spending of vast sums of money, a university needs an administration strong enough to handle such matters as these, and to handle them effectively.) I have tried to keep in mind Newman's conception of the balance of power and work within the university: The university for the advancement of knowledge and thus for the world; the college for the pursuit of liberal studies by young men and women, the handing on of tradition, and the education of the heart and its affections. Lastly, I have suggested that a college and, for the occasion of the lectures of which these pages are in part a record, in part a revision, a Catholic college, can only vindicate itself and justify its self-proclaimed role if it applies to its own religious tradition in all its richness and variety the same quality of attention it gives to the enterprise of learning it shares with the rest of the university.

It is a piece of harmless vanity in me to hope, not that these words put together for the University of Toronto's 150th birthday and Saint Michael's College's 125th will be long remembered, but that what has been said may pass anonymously into the flood of talk about universities and in that way make some difference to how things are done and to the look of things.

Notes

I 'THE IDEA OF
A UNIVERSITY' REVISITED

1 John Henry Newman *An Essay in
Aid of a Grammar of Assent*,
London 1906 (1870), 78, 79.
2 John Henry Newman *The Idea of
a University Defined and Illus-
trated*, edited with Introduction
and Notes by I.T. Ker, Oxford
1976, 132. (This edition will be
referred to hereafter as *Idea*.)
3 *Idea*, 132.
4 *Idea*, 132, 133.
5 *The Autobiography of William
Cobbett*, edited by William
Reitzel, London 1947, 99, 100.
6 Ibid., 102, 103.
7 *The Letters and Diaries of

John Henry Newman*, edited by
Charles Stephen Dessain, London
1965, XVI, 155 (letter to Manuel
Johnson).
8 Ibid.
9 *Idea*, 97.
10 E.P. Roe *Barriers Burned Away*.
Published in 1872, it was enor-
mously successful. 'Ten years
after its first printing, a "limited"
edition of a hundred thousand
copies was immediately sold out.
... As late as the mid-1880s,
Matthew Arnold thought the
country was "nourished and
formed" by "a native author
called Roe," but the accused
considered this an odd judgment,
since "no critic has ever been so

daft as to call any of my books a classic." ' James D. Hart *The Popular Book. A History of America's Literary Taste*, New York 1950, 121.

11 *Idea*, 110, 111.

12 *Idea*, 145.

13 *Idea*, 187.

14 'There is as much want of simplicity in the idea of the creation of distinct species as in those of the creation [of] trees in full growth (whose seed [is] in themselves) or of rocks with fossils in them. I mean that it is as strange that monkeys should be so like men, with no historical connexion between them, as that there should be, or the notion that there was, no history or course of facts by which fossil bones got into rocks. ... I will either go the whole hog with Darwin, or, dispensing with time and history altogether, hold, not only the theory of distinct species, but that also of the creation of the fossil-bearing rocks.' Unpublished papers at the Birmingham Oratory, note of 9 December 1863.

15 *Idea*, 193.

16 *Idea*, 193, 194.

17 Cf. Helen Waddell *Medieval Latin Lyrics*, London 1930, and *The Wandering Scholars*, London 1934 (revision and enlargement of the edition of 1927) passim.

18 On the Jesuits in China there is a vast literature. See e.g. Arnold H. Rowbotham *Missionary and Mandarin*. The Jesuits at the Court of China, New York 1966 (1942); and François Bontinck *La Lutte autour de la Liturgie*

Chinoise, Louvain and Paris 1962.

19 *Idea*, 214.

20 *Idea*, 213. This is a view of China Newman shared with many contemporaries; cf., for example, Tennyson's 'Better fifty years of Europe than a cycle of Cathay' (*Locksley Hall* 1842).

II COLLEGES, UNIVERSITIES AND THE STATE

1 Hastings Rashdall *The Universities of Europe in the Middle Ages*, edited by F.M. Powicke and A.B. Emden, London 1936, vol. I, 2 (hereafter referred to as Rashdall).

2 James Boswell *The Life of Samuel Johnson*, London (Everyman) 1906, vol. I, 281.

3 Rashdall, vol. I, 3.

4 *Idea*, 5.

5 Rashdall, vol. I, 6.

6 Rashdall, vol. I, 14.

7 *An Anatomy of Oxford*, an anthology compiled by C. Day Lewis and Charles Fenby, London 1938, 90.

8 ' ... I ventured to address [Routh] somewhat as follows: "Mr. President, give me leave to ask you a question I have sometimes asked of aged persons, but never of any so aged or so learned as yourself. ... Every studious man, in the course of a long and thoughtful life, has had occasion to experience the special value of some one axiom or precept. Would you mind giving me the benefit of such a word of advice?" ... He bade me explain, – evidently to gain time. I quoted an instance.

He nodded and looked thoughtful. Presently he brightened up and said, "I think, sir, since you care for the advice of an old man, sir, you will find it a very good practice" – (here he looked me archly in the face), – "*always to verify your references*, sir!" ' Thus Burgon, then Fellow of Oriel, in John William Burgon *Lives of Twelve Good Men*, London 1888, vol. I, 73.

9 *Idea*, 244.

10 J.M. Cameron *Images of Authority*, New Haven 1966, ix, x.

11 Mark Pattison *Memoirs*, London 1885, 303.

12 Abraham Flexner *Universities: American, English, German*, New York 1968 (1930), 267.

13 Rashdall, vol. I, 499.

14 Rashdall, vol. I, 536-39.

15 Rashdall, vol. I, 519.

16 John Henry Newman *The Office and Work of Universities*, London 1856, 274. (Hereafter referred to as *Office*.)

17 *Office*, 344, 345.

18 *Office*, 352, 353.

19 John Henry Cardinal Newman *Apologia pro Vita Sua*, edited, with an Introduction and Notes, by Martin J. Svaglic, Oxford 1967, 213.

20 Cf. 'What is the justification of the modern American multiversity? History is one answer. Consistency with the surrounding society is another. Beyond that, it has few peers in the preservation and dissemination and examination of the eternal truths; no living peers in the search for new knowledge; and no peers in all history among institutions of higher learning in serving so many of the segments of an advancing civilization. Inconsistent internally as an institution it is consistently productive. Torn by change, it has the stability of freedom. Though it has not a single soul to call its own, its members pay their devotions to truth.' Clark Kerr *The Uses of the University*, New York 1966 (1964), 44, 45.

III THE CRISIS OF THE UNIVERSITY

1 Commission on Post-Secondary Education in Ontario: Draft Report, Toronto 1971, 10. I add as further rich examples: 'Toward finding better ways to work out our problems, we offer the Western Institute of Aviation for broadening the base of understanding, evolving a means of lifting up our eyes and objectives and, hopefully, realizing our mutual dependence in optimizing aviation services to people through the synergism of our efforts.' This is by an anonymous writer of advertising copy. And, from a periodical *Art Education*: 'In terms of arting, where the reference condition is not fixed or even known conceptually but rather something coming to being, what can we hope through our formative hermeneutic movement?' These examples were given in *The New Yorker* and cited from that periodical in *Encounter*, vol. XLVIII, February 1977.

2 See Alain Schnapp et Pierre Vidal-Naquet *Journal de la Commune Etudiante: Textes et Documents*

Novembre 1967–Juin 1968, Paris 1969. This is available in an abridged translation: *The French Student Uprising November 1967–June 1968*, translated by Maria Jolas, Boston 1971.

3 No anthology of the writings of English-speaking students in revolt has, so far as I know, been published, certainly nothing to compare with the compilation by Schnapp and Vidal-Naquet, but a casual study of student newspapers, posters, flyers, and pamphlets, will I am confident, sustain my generalization. Of course, there are many books that contain useful material. Much the most penetrating and useful is, in my view, John Searle *The Campus War*, Harmondsworth 1972.

4 *Office*, 72, 73.

5 *Office*, 112.

6 *Office*, 112, 113.

7 *Idea*, 421.

8 See Simone Pétrement *Simone Weil: A Life*, translated from the French by Raymond Rosenthal, New York 1976, 64ff.

9 Robert Paul Wolff *The Ideal of the University*, Boston 1970 (1969), 153.

10 Ibid. 152, 153.

11 Paul Goodman *Compulsory Miseducation* and *The Community*

of *Scholars*, New York 1964, 163.

12 Ibid. 168.

IV SOME PROPOSALS FOR CHANGE AND REFORM

1 Flexner, *Universities*, 267.

2 *Socrates: A Source Book*, compiled and in part translated by John Ferguson, London 1970, 17.

3 On the idea of 'story' as a fundamental category of understanding, see Brian Wicker *The Story-Shaped World*, Notre Dame and London 1975.

4 Adam Smith *An Inquiry into the Nature and Causes of the Wealth of Nations*, Edinburgh 1811 (1776), vol. III, 172, 173 (Bk. V, ch. i, art. 2).

5 Pattison, *Memoirs*, 179.

6 Christopher Jencks and David Riesman *The Academic Revolution*, New York 1968, 405.

7 See e.g. *American Catholics and the Intellectual Life*, Chicago 1956.

8 See his *Luther: Right or Wrong?* New York and Minneapolis 1969.

9 Jencks and Riesman, *The Academic Revolution*, 356.

10 *Summa Theologiae*, $II^a II^{ae}$ Quaestio xl.

11 Peter Levi S.J. *In Memory of David Jones*, London 1975 5-11.